GREEN SMOOTHIE JOY
FOR NUTRIBULLET

GREEN SMOOTHIE JOY
FOR NUTRIBULLET

CRESSIDA ELIAS

Skyhorse Publishing

Skyhorse Publishing books may be purchased in bulk at special discounts for sales promotion, corporate gifts, fund-raising, or educational purposes. Special editions can also be created to specifications. For details, contact the Special Sales Department, Skyhorse Publishing, 307 West 36th Street, 11th Floor, New York, NY 10018 or info@skyhorsepublishing.com.

Skyhorse® and Skyhorse Publishing® are registered trademarks of Skyhorse Publishing, Inc.®, a Delaware corporation.

www.skyhorsepublishing.com

Library of Congress Cataloging-in-Publication Data:
Elias, C., author.
  Green smoothie joy for Nutribullet / Cressida Elias.
     pages cm
  Includes index.
  ISBN 978-1-63450-700-4 (hardcover : alk. paper) 1. Smoothies (Beverages) 2. Vegetable juices. 3. Health. 4. Functional foods. I. Title.
  TX817.S636E45 2015
  641.8'75--dc23

10 9 8 7 6 5 4 3 2 1

Print ISBN: 978-1-63450-700-4
Ebook ISBN: 978-1-63450-870-4

Printed in China

CONTENTS

7	Introduction
10	The Difference between Juicing and Blending
13	Blenders and Juicers
14	The Origin of Smoothies and the Green Smoothie
15	Using Frozen Fruit
16	Basic Ingredients and Essential Tips for Making Green Smoothies
19	Herbs and Seeds
22	Suggested Superfoods
24	About Milks: Buy or Make Your Own?
26	List of Fat-Burning Foods and Using Smoothies for Weight Loss
32	Other Fruits and Veggies and Their Nutritional Value
34	Vitamin and Mineral List
37	Extra Protein
38	Extra Tips for Smoothies
39	Ingredient Measurements in the Recipes
41	THE RECIPES
89	JUICE IT, SMOOTH IT RECIPES
111	SOME FRUITY, SOME YOGURTY SMOOTHIES
129	FILL UP AND GO GREEN SMOOTHIES
139	TIME CRUNCHED SMOOTHIES
141	VERY SWEET NAUGHTY SMOOTHIES
151	SEEDY SMOOTHIES
152	FRUIT-FREE SMOOTHIES
153	VERY NUTTY SMOOTHIES
154	SPECIFIC HEALTH SMOOTHIES
157	Conversion Chart
159	Resources
164	Recipe Index
166	Notes

INTRODUCTION

We are more aware than ever of the reasons why we should eat healthy. And we know that whatever we put into our bodies we are going to get out of them in terms of energy and health benefits.

But with our busy lifestyles, it is often very hard to eat good food on the go and most of us tend to pick up fast food, unhealthy snacks, or packaged food to save time. Getting that "five a day" serving of fruit and veggies can prove to be a difficult task!

But, just adding one large handful of spinach into your NutriBullet will add some bright green and a lot of nutrition to your smoothie! But if you took the same amount and added it to a salad instead—well, you would probably find it hard to munch through it all in one sitting!

Some people add extra ingredients such as protein powders or oats to make a satisfying meal out of a smoothie, saving cooking time! Some people just use greens and fruit for a mealtime smoothie and find it perfectly nourishing.

You may think that drinking several cups of store-bought fruit juice from the supermarket or café should supply your body with enough vitamins. However, most of these juices have added sugar or sweeteners, or are from concentrate, or have colors and "natural flavors" added, and have all been pasteurized.

To explain briefly:

Sugar can come in a variety of forms such as cane sugar, white sugar, beet sugar, corn syrup, dextrose, fructose, succanat, sucrose, and so on. Taken in excess, these forms of sugar can lead to problems with increased insulin (a hormone) levels in your body which in turn affects your blood sugar levels. Too much insulin creates insulin resistance, which is associated with obesity, fatigue, high blood pressure, diabetes, and other diseases. Also, excessive ingestion of these sugars will exhaust your pancreas and adrenal function. Still want your sugary fruit juice?

Artificial sweeteners are not recommended—natural sweeteners such as stevia and xylitol, if you must have them, are recommended instead.

Obviously, many colors and "natural flavors" in store-bought juice are artificial—some people are particularly sensitive to them—and they are not something you want (or need) to be taking when you are going for extra nutrition!

Pasteurization – normal or flash (meaning very fast) kills bacteria and prolongs the life of the juice (important for supermarkets) but this process can also cause a loss of nutrients and important enzymes.

Concentrated – this is when a fruit is squeezed, the water taken out of it so it can be transported more easily, then the water added back later. Micronutrients such as antioxidants are thought to be lost in this process.

So to *really* get the most out of your fruits and veggies, and unless you can go to a juice bar and watch them make your juice, you need to make your own and drink it as soon as possible while completely fresh. But remember *only* juicing will mean you miss out on all the essential fiber in the fruit and vegetables. If you use a NutriBullet, your smoothies will be very smooth and by adding more water you can make them more juice-like if you prefer without sacrificing the fiber which will slow down the release of the natural sugars into your body.

The question has been raised as to whether green smoothie enthusiasts drink too *many* greens and that this could become toxic to the body. There is no evidence that anyone has become sick from drinking nutrient-filled smoothies, however, everything in moderation. If you consumed only green smoothies every day then your diet would not be balanced and you would be creating other health problems for yourself—but this is just common sense.

This book has been created to celebrate the outstanding ability of the NutriBullet blender to create the smoothest smoothies which you can blend and go. The recipes are the same as in the original *Green Smoothie Joy* book but have been modified for the tall cup (24oz) plus I have included an additional 12 smoothies at the end of the book to complement the power of the NutriBullet. These are Seedy Smoothies, Fruit-Free Smoothies, Very Nutty Smoothies, and Specific Health Smoothies.

I hope you find all the recipes useful in your pursuit of greater health and renewed energy.

A FEW GREEN SMOOTHIE BENEFITS

- They can help detox and cleanse your body to generally improve your health or help heal conditions such as acne.

- Smoothies give real energy kicks and make a nice caffeine replacement.

- They are fast and easy to make and you can blend and go. You can also make and store them in the fridge for later in the day. They don't really taste as good the next day if you want to keep it but some people do this.

- You can pack a smoothie with different fruits and veggies you probably would not eat all in one day.

- Kids enjoy making them and drinking them, so you can hide some veggies under the taste of their favorite fruits.

- They are packed with enzymes and vitamins. The essential nutrient in greens (chlorophyll) helps to purify your blood and helps to eliminate bad breath and body odor and is great for anemia.

- The antioxidants and phytochemicals present in veggies give you energy for a healthy snack or a meal replacement if you are dieting.

- Greens are alkaline; this is great for your health as ingesting alkaline food will help balance your acid/alkaline level, which can help prevent or heal many different health problems.

THE DIFFERENCE BETWEEN JUICING AND BLENDING

Some people prefer to juice their raw food and others prefer a blended smoothie. They are both nutritious and I will try to explain in brief the benefits of both.

If you put veggies and fruit in a juicer, you will leave the fiber and pulp behind and just get a liquid full of vitamins, enzymes, and lots of micronutrients, including the raw food "x factor" that will definitely give you a buzz. Some people prefer the liquid because the body is able to absorb the nutrients in minutes rather than a couple of hours because there is no fiber or pulp to slow down digestion.

If you throw fruit and greens into a blender then you will be getting a more fulfilling drink because the "meat" of the food is still in the drink, but the cell walls have been broken down to a more digestible (liquid) form that you couldn't accomplish on your own unless you chewed for hours! So you will still benefit from all the nutrients that the fruit or vegetable has to offer. However, drink your smoothie slowly as your body still needs time to digest the fiber and drinking them too quickly can cause bloating. Rest assured that once you start sipping a green smoothie, your body will begin absorbing the nutrients immediately. Fiber is important for your body as it helps the elimination of waste, which is vital for cleaning out your colon. Drinking two or three green smoothies a day will fill you up and supply your body with essential vitamins and minerals.

Just having one juice and one smoothie a day can get you incredible results—increased health, vitality, and weight loss.

Bear in mind that if you come across a smoothie recipe that requires juice—make the juice yourself. That way you can be assured of its freshness.

Fruits are considered "cleansing" and veggies are "nourishing," so ideally you'll want to get both fruit and veggies into your smoothies. But sometimes you may just crave a fruity snack or treat—nothing wrong with that!

Generally, green smoothies are approximately 60 percent fruit and 40 percent vegetables, which makes them taste a lot better than 100 percent vegetable juices because the fruit content makes them a bit sweeter.

However, once you get used to the "green" taste, you can reduce the fruit and increase the vegetables in the smoothie to rebuild and regenerate your body faster. Try and aim for a 80:20 split or even less fruit, particularly if you are sensitive to sugar or have yeast and candida problems. Fruit sugar will raise your blood sugar levels so I generally recommend you use mostly low sugar fruit such as berries rather than lots of very sweet fruit such as grapes and bananas.

NutriBullet recommends 50 percent leafy greens and 50 percent fruit or veggies plus a handful of nuts or seeds as a "boost." All this plus the water should not go over the "MAX" line.

For a sweeter taste without using fruit, try a carrot—juice it or add it whole to the blender. You will be surprised at how sweet it is!

Some people experience an unpleasant "detox" feeling when starting to juice or blend for the first time. This feeling will pass after a short while, and certainly blending greens rather than simply juicing them will minimize this effect as the absorption rate is a little slower. That is why some people prefer green smoothies over green juices.

Most green smoothie enthusiasts recommend you rotate your green veggies to ensure a balanced vegetable intake.

One more reason some people favor smoothies—the blender is easier to clean! Juicers usually have several parts, but a blender just has a jug that can be washed quickly. If you are rushing out the door you can definitely throw your ingredients into a blender, whizz it, pour, and run out of the house with minimal mess left behind.

A NutriBullet is extremely easy to use and better than a normal blender because it is smaller and the blender cup can be drunk from and comes with a lid, so you can literally blend and go.

However, if you are juicing you will have to clean the juicer, but if you rinse the parts straight away, the clean-up isn't too time-consuming. My juicer has only five parts that come apart easily and can be replaced without much hassle.

BLENDERS AND JUICERS

One of the best blenders to come to market recently is the NutriBullet. At a reasonable price, you get a fast, light blender with a fantastic chopping action, plus several cups and lids. Because the blender is fast with unique blades, and generally smaller than other blenders, blending is quick and you can crush ice, seeds, and nuts into smooth drinks in less time. There is only one speed so you don't have to worry about a dial or different switches. You just put the cup on the blender and switch on. You can of course add home-made juices to the NutriBullet instead of water. For this you will need a juicer.

Juicers can be bought separately or can come with a blender. These days, juicers are pretty easy to clean with only a few parts to assemble. I use a Philips brand centrifugal juicer, and although it is a little more bulky than a blender, it does a good job.

I recommend a centrifugal juicer—these are high-speed, cheap, and juice very quickly. Some people prefer a masticating juicer or twin-gear one, which basically juices at low speeds by crushing, and gets more juice out of a vegetable than a centrifugal one. These juicers also don't aerate the juice like the centrifugal ones, meaning you can keep the juice in the fridge longer before it spoils. The high-speed juicers will make juice that you should drink straight away. Also, some people say the high speed juicers heat the juice and reduce the enzyme activity of it. I personally haven't found this to be a problem but I suggest you look into it if you are concerned.

THE ORIGIN OF SMOOTHIES AND THE GREEN SMOOTHIE

Smoothies have actually been around since the 1930s when the first Waring blender was invented. Smoothies then were just blended fruit and ice, but adding yogurt or milk became more popular in the '60s and '70s. Thereafter, with the help of the growing fitness industry, smoothies became even more popular and all sorts of new ingredients were added to the mix—including protein powder, wheatgrass, etc.

In the last few years green smoothies have been gaining a lot of popularity due to their incredible health benefits (and great taste!). They were popularized by raw food diet practitioner Victoria Boutenko. She was interested in how eating large amounts of green leafy vegetables could have an effect on her family's health.

She learned that chimpanzees who have an almost identical DNA structure to humans, were more resistant to common diseases such as cancer, AIDS, and heart disease. She discovered that while the standard US diet was comprised of only 3 percent green veggies, in the diet of a chimpanzee green veggies amounted to a whopping 39 percent. Thus, Victoria started to make smoothies with lots of veggies to increase the greens in her diet (blending the greens down meant you could drink a lot more than you would be able to eat). And so the Green Smoothie was born.

Dr. Ann Wigmore, who was an early pioneer of a raw and natural food diet, made a comparison between a molecule of chlorophyll (from green leafy veggies) to a molecule of human blood—the idea being that ingesting chlorophyll is like receiving a healthy blood transfusion!

Of course, the green smoothie became very popular, not least because it was easy to drink your daily dose of green veggies, but also because kids love them, and people see huge health benefits from drinking them—from increased health and energy to weight loss.

There are so many combinations you can make with fruit and veggies that you won't ever get bored. It doesn't matter if you stick to the same few fruit and veggies if you are reliant on what your local farm shop and superstore have in stock. You can still add other ingredients like oats or flax seed, etc. for different tastes and nutritional needs.

USING FROZEN FRUIT

You can freeze fresh fruit or buy frozen packaged fruit (I love using frozen berries, for example) and use these in a smoothie—the frozen fruit creates a cool, thicker smoothie and you probably won't need to add extra ice. Bananas are particularly good frozen—peel them when they are ripe and full of vitamins and minerals, not when they are hard and just starchy—slice them, freeze on a bit of foil then store in the freezer in a freezer bag or container. Now you can add a few slices of banana each morning instead of having to use a whole one each time, if you wish to change the amount of fruit in your smoothies.

For other large fruits like melons, chop them up as well and freeze on a plate or some foil first before putting them all together in a bag and leaving in the freezer.

BASIC INGREDIENTS AND ESSENTIAL TIPS FOR MAKING GREEN SMOOTHIES

Healthy smoothies need a base for creaminess, some liquid, then the fruit and/or veggies, plus added ingredients for extra nutrition.

For the base, most green and other smoothie makers use either banana, avocado, and/or mango or papaya to make them creamy. For other fruit smoothies you can use yogurt for a creamy texture and for extra bulk and nutrition you can add oats to any smoothie. Alternately, nuts make a great base as they are extremely creamy when you blend them with some water.

Bananas are great when they are ripe. That is when they have a few black and brown spots on them and are full of vitamins and minerals. They contain fiber, vitamin A, C, E, K, thiamine, riboflavin, niacin, B6, folate, B12, and pantothenic acid. A banana will really add a sweeter taste to your smoothie and cover up a lot of the green taste. It may also solidify after an hour or so and you could serve up a green smoothie dessert!

To make green smoothies more palatable for kids, add more banana, mango, pineapple or berries—the sweetness will keep the greens hidden.

For other fruit smoothies you can use yogurt, cream, or creme fraiche for a creamy texture. Some people prefer not to use dairy for health reasons and I personally have chosen to go dairy free for weight loss and as a healthier choice but please do your own research on this subject. For extra bulk and nutrition you can also add oats to any smoothie.

If you want to avoid fruit, then avocados give a thick texture to a smoothie and provide vital nutrients and phytochemicals—just make sure they are ripe (not black and dented).

Using mango and/or pineapple and coconut milk together will give you a tropical taste to any smoothie.

For a boost to the nutritional value of a smoothie, you can add wheatgrass powder, whey, or other protein powders, maca, flax seeds, or other green powders like spirulina. Just adding one of these will add more "energy" to the smoothie, so have a couple handy (see chapter on superfoods).

You can try other liquids in your smoothie other than cow's milk and water. Almond milk, hemp milk, juiced

A NOTE ON AVOCADOS AND FAT CONTENT

I use avocados in most of the recipes because they are great for adding thickness to a smoothie and are nutrient-dense. They contain all 18 essential amino acids and thus are a complete protein that is easy to digest. They also contain "healthy fat" which boosts the so-called "good" cholesterol, which helps protect against free radical damage and diabetes. They are rich in carotenoids (for eye health) and are anti-inflammatory. The main fat in avocados is oleic acid, which actually is shown to improve heart health. They also contain many omega-3 fatty acids, which are known to lower risk of heart disease. The fat content that you may be worried about is the *good* kind of fat!

If you are starting a healthy diet, trying to lose weight, or going "raw," one or two avocados a day can actually help you make the transition as they will fill you up and curb your cravings. My advice is to simply listen to your body. Limit your bad fat intake or give it up altogether. You can easily adjust the amount of avocado you use in a green smoothie according to your needs—less if you are just having a snack smoothie, more if you are using it as a meal replacement. I love the taste of avocado in my smoothies but if you don't, then decrease the amount to a quarter of an avocado and add more fruit.

veggies or fruit, and coconut milk as suggested above, will all add a different taste and consistency.

Green smoothie enthusiasts will go out looking for green leaves in gardens themselves and pick edible leaves and blend them up. You really do have to know what is edible and what is not to do this. I would advise you not to do this unless you are 110 percent sure of what you are picking, as some leaves are poisonous. I would stick to what you can get locally from markets and shops and keep an eye out for in-season produce to change up your routine. There will not be any recipes in this book with hard-to-find ingredients!

Other ingredients to have handy are honey, maple syrup, the sugar substitute xylitol, or the sweet herb stevia. However you should only need these if you are not using much fruit but you wish to have a little sweetness to your smoothie. The juice of carrot, beetroot, pomegranate or extra berries or banana should give you enough sweetness without resorting to sweeteners.

HERBS AND SEEDS

Herbal teas are a great addition to smoothies. You could try brewing some ginger tea, chamomile tea, nettle tea, or green tea and adding the liquid to reach the desired consistency. Alternately, you can find fresh herbs from your local store and add them directly to your smoothie!

Basil goes well with mango or with apples, carrots, and berries.

Chia seed is a member of the mint family and is an very old food used in the diet of the Mayan, Aztec, and Southwest Native American people. Chia is the highest plant source of omega-3, which is an essential fat we don't get enough of in the Western diet, so by adding just a tablespoon to your smoothies you will be doing yourself a world of good. It also helps thicken a thin smoothie instead of using extra banana or avocado, etc. If you get the seed already milled then you won't need to worry about an extra crunch in your smoothie.

Cilantro (also called coriander) is good with pineapple, strawberries, and bananas and is known for its great health benefits—including removing toxic metals from the body, cleansing the liver, acting as a natural antiseptic, and providing a good source of iron, vitamin C, and magnesium.

Flax seed (or linseed) is high in fiber, phytochemicals, and omega-3. It is best if this is already milled. There is a small amount of cyanide in flax seed; however, it appears in such low amounts that it's not a health concern—usually flax seed consumption is about 1 or 2 tablespoons a day.

Hemp seeds are another source of omega-3, vitamins, protein, and minerals. Again, find it milled as it's easier to blend.

Mint is great with melon, kiwi, or strawberries and gives the smoothie a little extra freshness to it. Mint contains vitamins A, C, and B2 and various essential minerals such as manganese, copper, iron, etc.

Parsley is great in green smoothies—it really packs a good vitamin punch with iron, protein, calcium, beta-carotene, and other trace vitamins and minerals such as magnesium, potassium, and zinc. It's very low in calories but is high in fiber. As the herb is quite pungent it is best to use it sparingly and combine it with other greens such as kale and spinach. Fruits that go with parsley are pear with kiwi or pineapple and mango with oranges.

Pumpkin seeds are packed with fiber, vitamins, and minerals and also the free radical-fighting antioxidants.

They also contain protein so they're great in a mealtime smoothie.

Sprouted seeds are a great source of nutrition—and you can even sprout your own if you feel ambitious. Alfalfa, broccoli, lentil, mung bean, wheatgrass, and pea-sprouted seeds are just some examples.

They contain many nutrients such as vitamins, protein, minerals, and enzymes. They have fiber and are alkalizing for your body, which is great for your health. They contain both iron and vitamin C and give your immune system a good kick.

Sunflower seeds are quite nutty and high in calories full of good nutrients such as vitamins, particularly vitamin E, minerals, and of course antioxidants. They also are a good protein source. Various benefits of eating these seeds are: a reduced blood sugar level, decrease in anxiety, and lower LDL cholesterol levels.

Nuts are a great way of boosting the nutrition in a smoothie as they contain protein and other nutrients such as zinc and vitamin E and can make your smoothies creamy without using bananas and avocados if you don't wish to.

It's a good idea to first soak nuts and seeds for a few hours or overnight before using them in smoothies. They will blend better, plus more of their nutrition is released with soaking.

SUGGESTED SUPERFOODS

A superfood is a term to describe foods that are densely packed with nutrients and should be included in your diet. I often use a ready-made powder comprised of something like green barley grass or wheatgrass. However, if you are juicing and blending lots of fruit and veggies every day you should not really need extra superfood powder. That said, some people might need an extra boost. It's also handy if you are out of green veggies or just want to make something fruity but add a little "green."

There is a huge list of foods now that are generally referred to as "super," but here are some that you can easily find and include in a smoothie:

BLUEBERRIES
High in fiber and antioxidants, blueberries are a top superfood.

BLUE-GREEN ALGAE
Comes in powder form and is the richest source of chlorophyll known to man. It is a substance that basically cleans your blood and detoxifies. Also a great source of protein, beta-carotene, and B12.

BRAZIL NUTS
A great way to get a good dose of selenium, zinc, protein, magnesium, and thiamine. You can throw a couple of these into the blender every now and then and they will smooth out well. I have seen it recommended that you don't eat more than 1 or 2 brazil nuts a day because of their high selenium content; they can become toxic in high doses, and also raise your LDL cholesterol.

CACAO
Raw chocolate, an extremely rich antioxidant and packed with iron, magnesium, and chromium as well. It is said to raise your mood, lower cholesterol, and improve the circulation of your blood. Cacao also contains phenethylamine which is reported to create greater focus and make you more alert. The phytochemicals in cacao are said to be an aphrodisiac. Bear in mind it does contain some caffeine as well. You can usually get cacao nibs or powder in your local health store. Will make your smoothie chocolatey!

COCONUT
Good for energy, burning fat, and is a good source of fiber, iron, and manganese. It is also reported to improve your thyroid function.

GUAVA
This is packed full of vitamin C, plus fiber, potassium, manganese, and folic acid.

MACA

Often referred to as Incan superfood, it has been used for thousands of years by Andean societies to nourish and heal. Benefits include increased stamina, endurance, and libido, and it is also said to stimulate tired adrenals and the entire endocrine system to restore vitality. It contains amino acids, minerals, vitamins, alkaloids, and sterols (great for body builders!). It has a vanilla/caramel taste and is great in smoothies.

MESQUITE POWDER

Some people put this in their smoothies. It is ground from the pods in the mesquite plant and has been eaten for thousands of years by Native Americans. It is rich in protein, fiber, potassium, iron, zinc, calcium, and lysine, and is apparently very good at balancing blood sugar because the sugar within it is a fructose and does not require insulin to metabolise it.

As a side note, if you are diabetic or hypoglycemic, green smoothies can help your condition. You can stick to just veggies, tomato, and avocado, no fruit or very low sugar fruit, and add milled flax seed, flax seed oil, or hemp seed oil to your smoothies, which helps slow down the digestion and release of sugars.

POMEGRANATE

Full of antioxidants as well and the seeds contain fiber. Its benefits include: prevention of blood clots, reported to be a natural cure for prostate cancer, can prevent heart problems, reduces diarrhea, reduces plaque in arteries, lowers blood pressure, and many more.

RASPBERRIES

High in fiber, antioxidants, and other nutrients.

SPIRULINA

This is a type of blue-green algae and a wonderful source of protein, essential fatty acids, minerals, and vitamins. The iron is beneficial for those with anemia. It is said to help with weight loss, detoxify your body, improve blood sugar problems, remove toxic metals from the body, and lower cholesterol, among other benefits.

WHEATGRASS

This is good for chlorophyll, enzymes, amino acids, minerals, and vitamins. Benefits include increasing red blood cell count, lowering blood pressure, helping to detoxify the body, neutralizing toxins, and alkalizing the body. It will strengthen your cells, is said to restore fertility, turn gray hair to normal color, and even freshen your breath!

This is just a short list of the many superfoods available to you. If you check out your local health food store you will be sure to find various superfoods in powder form that will provide your smoothie with that extra nutrient boost.

ABOUT MILKS: BUY OR MAKE YOUR OWN?

Adding milk is a great option for your smoothies. It will help create a creamier and thicker consistency than just adding water. So go ahead and happily add some organic cow's milk, goat milk, hemp seed milk, or almond milk to your next creation.

Cow's milk has come under scrutiny recently with some health professionals now saying it's bad for us and only baby cows should drink it! However, some health practitioners say that organic raw milk is fine to drink because it is unpasteurised and the healthy bacteria and enzymes are still intact and no artificial growth hormones are present. I have seen reports of dairy being linked to cancer as well, so I wouldn't want to recommend it but if you do use it, don't go overboard. Goat's milk is said to be much healthier. Do your own research but I personally gave up dairy to lose extra weight and be healthier and didn't find it hard at all as I use coconut milk, almond milk, and water instead. This book does have yogurt smoothie recipes because I figured everyone wants a treat sometimes and if probiotic yogurts are used, you will get a good dose of healthy bacteria!

When you buy almonds, make sure they are the sweet variety that have been pasteurized, as opposed to raw almonds—these are a safer choice.

You can use brazil nut milk in moderation—as aforementioned, brazil nuts can be toxic is large doses. I suggest making a small amount of brazil nut milk and using sparingly; alternatively, pop a brazil nut or two in your smoothie once a day or every now and then.

Hemp seeds are great for protein as they contain eight amino acids and therefore are a "complete" protein. They contain a high amount of omega-3 fatty acids, vitamins, and minerals. Hemp milk I find, though, is an acquired taste!

Pumpkin seeds also make a good milk.

YOU CAN FIND OAT, NUT, AND SEED MILKS IN THE STORE, BUT IF YOU WANT TO MAKE YOUR OWN, THEN USE THIS PROCEDURE:

- Soak your nuts overnight before blending. (Hemp seeds don't need soaking; just rinse). Rinse the soaked seeds or nuts.

- Take a cup of your choice of seeds or nuts.

- Put in the NutriBullet and add three to four cups of filtered or pure water.

- Add one or two dates or a little honey, xylitol, stevia, agave nectar, or cinnamon plus a little vanilla extract—these are all optional depending on your taste.

- Blend and then pour through a sieve or strainer and for even better straining, put through a cheesecloth.

- This will give you a thick milk.

- For a thinner consistency, add more water in the original mix or blend with the strained milk.

- Refrigerate and store as normal milk but shake before use in case of separation.

LIST OF FAT-BURNING FOODS AND USING SMOOTHIES FOR WEIGHT LOSS

Without a doubt you can lose weight drinking green smoothies! Replace your daily snacks of cookies, potato chips, or other unhealthy foods with a smoothie for a great start to healthy eating and weight loss.

I lost approximately seven pounds in two weeks just from replacing breakfast or lunch with a green smoothie. I usually made enough for two or three glasses so what I didn't consume at that meal-time I had later as a snack. The great thing about smoothies is that once you start drinking them you will notice that you won't feel so hungry for unhealthy snacks, your energy will last longer, and it will become even easier to cut back on breakfast or lunch. You will probably be ready for a good evening meal though—make sure it's healthy!

To accelerate your fat burning, try fat-burning foods in your smoothies—check out the following list:

APPLES

They are full of soluble fiber called pectin which help you feel fuller for longer.

Apples also contain Vitamin C.

APRICOTS

Rich in fiber, apricots help you feel fuller longer and will help to lower blood cholesterol levels. They contain a lot of beta-carotene, which helps mop up free radicals and improve your immune system.

BEETS

Beets are a natural diuretic—this means they will help flush out excess water weight or fluid. They have iron, fiber, and natural chlorine, which will help rinse toxins and fats out of your body. Because of the iron content in beets they are a great food for people with anemia.

BROCCOLI

Broccoli is full of fiber as well, and rich in vitamin C, which will dilute the fat and make it easier to flush from your body. Contains several B vitamins, calcium, iron, beta-carotene, and can help lower blood pressure and detox your liver. Use only a few florets per smoothie because it is quite bitter tasting—you can juice it first and add it for extra "green."

BLACKBERRIES

Full of fiber, vitamin C, and other nutrients.

BLUEBERRIES

Blueberries are considered a great stomach fat fighter. They are full of phytonutrients, antioxidants, and are low-calorie if you are being careful. They are a low-sugar fruit, so they are a good option if you are sensitive to sugar.

CABBAGE

Sulfur and iodine in cabbage help cleanse your stomach and intestines. Cabbage also contains calcium and vitamin C.

CANTALOUPE

Good for vitamin A and C, potassium, vitamin B6, dietary fiber, folate, and niacin (vitamin B3), and fiber.

CARROTS

Makes a very sweet juice to add to smoothies, they are high in vitamin A and are a good detoxifier, and help your liver and guts function smoothly.

CELERY

This will eliminate carbon dioxide from your system and its pure form of calcium will feed your endocrine system. Hormones from this part of your body help to break up fats. Contains magnesium and iron and is a natural diuretic.

CHERRIES

Obviously remove the stone before blending! They are supposed to reduce pain and inflammation and contain anthocyanin which is said to contribute to belly fat reduction.

CHIVES

Help with weight loss due to their high chromium content. Chromium is a nutrient that improves the good functioning of insulin in the bloodstream. Basically the more stable your insulin, the more stable your blood sugar levels and the more stable your energy is, leading to less cravings!

CRANBERRIES

Low in sugar, plus great for the urinary and digestive tract. Great for fighting cellulite and detoxifying your body.

CUCUMBERS

A great fat-burner because as a diuretic, they will encourage the removal of waste fluids from your body. They also have good amounts of silica and sulfur to stimulate the kidneys to flush out uric acid in the body. Good for nails, skin, and hair, and can reduce blood pressure.

DANDELION GREENS

Dandelion leaves and roots are used to treat various ailments and boost health by Europeans, Asians, and Native Americans. The greens stimulate the liver, kidneys, and digestion, and act as a diuretic.

GOJI BERRIES

Fantastic for antioxidants and contain protein, essential minerals, and amino acids. You can buy these dried. Great for blood building and the immune system.

GRAPEFRUIT

Grapefruit will help the body's insulin levels and contribute to a fat-loss regime.

GREEN BEANS

Low in calories, rich in minerals. Improve liver, kidney, and lung functions. Green beans have vitamin C and iron, which both fight fat.

HONEYDEW MELON

Great for fiber and for high water content, so will boost your hydration on a hot day, plus deliver vitamins and minerals to your body.

JUNIPER BERRIES

Help eliminate excess water retention and improve digestion. They are also anti-inflammatory! **Not to be consumed by pregnant women or women wishing to conceive as juniper can cause uterine contractions.**

KALE

Kale is a member of the same family as Brussels sprouts and broccoli. Very high in fiber and contains many nutrients, so great for dieters.

LETTUCE

Full of vitamins and minerals and good for your metabolism with thermogenic properties. (Thermogenic fruits and veggies are low in calories but require a lot of energy to digest, thus raising your metabolism after you eat them, which helps you burn more fat.)

LEMONS

A squeeze of lemon is great for breaking down fat and cleansing the body.

LIMES

Packed with fat-fighting vitamin C!

MANGO

Packed with fiber but low in calories, a good source of beta-carotene and vitamin C.

NECTARINE

Has protein, fiber, and is full of nutrients. The calcium, magnesium, and potassium promote fluid balance, so they are good for weight loss.

OATMEAL

Adding some oatmeal to a smoothie can help you lose weight as it is high in fiber, which will help stabilize your blood sugar, so you are less likely to snack on unhealthy snacks.

ORANGE

Great for their high vitamin C content and fiber.

PAPAYA

Papaya is fat-free and contains fiber, A, C, potassium, calcium, iron, thiamine, riboflavin, and niacin. Also contains the enzyme peptin, which helps dissolve fat in the body. Please buy organic as papaya is often genetically modified.

PEACHES

Packed with vitamins and nutrients and fiber. They are full of fiber, which makes them filling.

PEARS

Contain a very high fiber content with vitamin C and calcium.

PINEAPPLE

Pineapples contain the enzyme bromelain, which helps digest protein and is also anti-inflammatory. They are also a good source of fiber, thiamine, vitamin B6, copper, vitamin c, and manganese.

PUMPKIN SEEDS

Also called pepitas, these are delicious crunchy snacks that are rich in manganese, tryptophan, magnesium, and phosphorus. They are thought to be anti-inflammatory agents as well.

RASPBERRIES

The raspberry is a good fat buster because of its high fiber content and low sugar level. The pectin in raspberries will help prevent too much fat from being absorbed into your cells, thus helping weight loss.

SPINACH

Packed with iron, it will boost your metabolism when eaten regularly and will promote better liver function.

STRAWBERRIES

Packed with powerful antioxidants, plus they also help reduce inflammation and increase metabolism. Can help control blood sugar levels.

TOMATO

Good vitamin C content plus contains phytochemicals that produce carnitine. Carnitine helps to break down fat inside your body so it can be used for energy.

WATERMELON

Contains loads of fiber and minerals and is great for your metabolism. Watermelons will hydrate you due to their high water content making them great for smoothies.

OTHER FRUITS AND VEGGIES AND THEIR NUTRITIONAL VALUE

AVOCADO

My favorite choice in green smoothies, they are high in protein, potassium, fiber, many vitamins including A, E, C, B6, and K, and healthy unsaturated fats for sustained energy.

BANANAS

Contain vitamins, minerals, and antioxidants. Particularly known for their high fiber, high potassium, vitamin C, and B6 content. Great for a quick energy boost due to their simple sugars content.

COCONUT

Useful in smoothies as water or milk. Loaded with antioxidant properties, it helps the body with many functions including digestion, cell building, sugar levels, weight loss, and metabolism—and it's antibacterial too. It has a higher concentration of electrolytes than any other food. So great for hydration!

DATES

Contain many vitamins and minerals, particularly high in fiber, iron, potassium, and antioxidant beta-carotene.

FENNEL

Good for fiber, vitamins, minerals, and antioxidants.

GINGER

Anti-inflammatory and antibacterial. Helps reduce nausea, migraines, and diarrhea (caused by e. coli). It contains nutrients including vitamins B5 and B6, potassium, magnesium, and manganese.

GRAPES

Rich in resveratrol, which is a powerful antioxidant, but but they are very sweet, so be careful if you have a sugar problem.

PASSION FRUIT

Very good source of antioxidants, fiber, vitamins, and minerals, particularly vitamins C, A, and potassium.

PRUNES

Very rich in vitamin A and antioxidants. Of course full of fiber and great for constipation!

KIWI

Great source of vitamin C and E, potassium, and folic acid. Good for blood pressure, heart health, immune system health, and digestion. Will help you feel relief from blockage and bloating.

RED CABBAGE
Lots of vitamin C and other vitamins and minerals plus fiber.

SWEET BELL PEPPERS

Rich source of vitamins and minerals particularly vitamin C in the red pepper, and all contain high vitamin A content. Capsaicin is an alkaloid present in these peppers, which is said to be good for cholesterol levels and is also anti-bacterial, and anti-carcinogenic, with beneficial properties for diabetics.

OTHER GREEN SMOOTHIE GREENS
COLLARD GREENS

A good source of phytonutrients that have anti-cancer properties. Great for vitamins A, K, and C and various minerals.

MUSTARD GREENS
Very high in vitamin K, and good for vitamins A and C, plus a high level of folates and fiber.

ROCKET OR ARUGULA LETTUCE
Rich in phytochemicals which fight various cancers such as breast, prostate, and ovarian. Contains minerals, particularly calcium and iron plus vitamin K and vitamin C.

ROMAINE LETTUCE
Very rich in vitamin A, plus folates, vitamin C and K, B vitamins, and iron.

SWISS CHARD LEAVES

A rich source of vitamins A, C, and K plus iron and omega-3 fatty acids. If regularly used, it is said to help iron deficient anemia, prevent osteoporosis and various heart diseases and some cancers.

TURNIP GREENS

Has high levels of antioxidants, vitamins A, C, E, calcium, and copper and is said to be useful for those with arthritis.

WATERCRESS
Great for vitamin A, C, and K, beta-carotene, and various minerals.

You will find many other green veggies in the supermarkets such as spring greens, bok choy, and so on. Feel free to experiment!

VITAMIN AND MINERAL LIST

I thought it might be beneficial to know the functions of various vitamins and minerals, as I have included approximate nutritional information in certain foods in previous chapters and also in each smoothie recipe. If you are looking to increase your intake of a certain vitamin or mineral, then you can choose a smoothie recipe or certain fruits and veggies accordingly. This list is by no means comprehensive; information can be found in more detail online, but for this book, it should be of some use!

A (RETINOL)
For vision, skin, bone, tooth growth, etc.

B1 (THIAMINE)
For good nerve function and metabolism.

B2 (RIBOFLAVIN)
For metabolism, eyes, and skin. Good for headaches.

B3 (NIACIN)
For metabolism, skin, nervous system, and digestion.

B6 (PYRIDOXINE)
For metabolism of amino and fatty acids and good for red blood cell production.

FOLATE
A water-soluble B vitamin that is needed to make DNA and create and maintain cell formation.

B12
Needed to create new cells, break down fatty and amino acids, and good for nerves.

C (ASCORBIC ACID)
Used for collagen creation, amino acid metabolism, great for iron absorption, your immune system, tired adrenals, and it's an antioxidant.

CALCIUM
Helps to form bones and teeth, and supports blood clotting.

CHLORIDE
Controls the flow of fluids in your blood vessels and tissues and helps regulate body acidity.

CHROMIUM
Helps support insulin and regulate blood sugar levels.

COPPER
Helps in the absorption of iron and the formation of hemoglobin.

D

Great for your immune system and for maintaining strong bones and muscles.

E

A great antioxidant, boosts your immune system and widens blood vessels to prevent unwanted blood clotting.

IODINE

Needed by the thyroid, which regulates growth and metabolism.

IRON

Important for energy, and an essential component of hemoglobin that carries oxygen throughout the body.

K

Extremely important in creating proteins that regulate blood clotting, and for bone strengthening.

MAGNESIUM

Used to maintain normal muscle and nerve function, good for the heart and relaxation. It helps keep your immune system healthy, bones strong, and can regulate sugar levels. Good for normal blood pressure and energy metabolism.

MANGANESE

Supports cell metabolism and protein digestion.

PHOSPHORUS

Essential for bone strength and for the formation of cells.

POTASSIUM

Works with sodium to help maintain water balance in your body, helps control blood pressure, heart rate, and helps with the utilization of energy in the body.

SODIUM

Balances your fluids and electrolytes and supports muscles and nerves.

SELENIUM

Is an antioxidant and helps prevent oxidation in the body.

ZINC

Essential for your immune system, human growth, and enzyme activity.

A NOTE ON THE VITAMIN CONTENT
AND NUTRITIONAL VALUE OF EACH RECIPE

Below each recipe there is a quick guide to the approximate nutritional value of the smoothie. Percent Daily Values are based on a diet of 2,000 calories but your diet may include more or less calories depending on your needs. "High" means that the nutrient is above 20 percent of the daily requirement. Iron is given as a percentage of the Percent Daily Value (PDV) However you can still use the information given to determine whether a smoothie is high in a certain nutrient.

The nutrition data is for the all the ingredients in the recipes and usually makes about 2 glasses of smoothie. For one glass just half the nutritional information.

EXTRA PROTEIN

If you are replacing a meal with a green smoothie, you may wish to add some extra protein in the form of protein powder or a superfood powder. You certainly don't have to, as you may find an avocado in your smoothie or nuts and hemp seeds provide you with all the protein you need. However some people may feel they need more depending on their age, weight, and activity level.

You might choose to use a whey protein powder—just make sure it is from a good organic source—I use a rice protein powder that is totally satisfying.

You can also throw in some oats for extra energy or protein. Oats are a powerhouse of phytonutrients and these, plus the fiber, help with high blood pressure, sugar level problems, bowel problems, and weight loss, as well as having anti-cancer properties.

EXTRA TIPS FOR SMOOTHIES

1. Need tips on getting your children to drink nutritious smoothies? This is quite simple—first make it sweet with banana and strawberries, *then* throw in the spinach or lettuce, and finally color it with blueberries, organic chocolate powder, or some raw cacao powder. Remember though—there is caffeine in the cacao and chocolate powder.

2. Add sparkling water for a different effect—both visually and on your taste buds!

3. If your smoothie didn't come out quite as creamy as you had hoped, add an avocado, a banana, or mango. You may also like to add some Greek yogurt with friendly bacteria or nuts such as cashews to make a creamier texture.

4. Make a green smoothie into a chocolate dessert by adding just greens, plain chocolate powder, avocado, and banana. Refrigerate and it will become like a mousse.

5. Remember to rotate your green veggies for better nutrition. Victoria Boutenko suggests that one should only mix green leaves with fruit, but if using other starchy vegetables such as broccoli, carrots, green beans, cabbage, etc., then it is best to keep fruit out of the smoothie as the combination may cause gas. Or, in my opinion, you can try juicing them and adding them to smoothies for extra vitmins, etc.

6. Add ice while blending to prevent the smoothie from warming up too quickly, or use some frozen fruit.

INGREDIENT MEASUREMENTS IN THE RECIPES

The ingredients have been edited from the original *Green Smoothie Joy* book to fit the tall cup of the NutriBullet. This cup provides a generous serving for one person and because the blender comes with lids and additional cups you can take one with you for the day. You can always decrease the ingredients and water to make a smaller smoothie and blend in one of their smaller cups. Always keep an eye on the Max Line on the cup as the recipes will just indicate what liquid to use and will assume you will fill the cup up to cover the fruit and veg to this line.

In this edition, I have included under each smoothie recipe just the list of main vitamins and minerals that you should expect to find in that recipe. I have decided to leave out the fat and calories contents because in general, nutritionists are now agreeing that losing weight and getting renewed energy and health is more about getting the right fat and enough calories from good food sources to keep you feeling satisfied, although out of interest you can refer to *Green Smoothie Joy* for this information. So you can happily use these smoothies for snacks or meal replacements, being aware of course that if you have a sugar imbalance or intolerance you would need to be careful of the fruit content of your smoothie.

A NOTE ON COOKED VEGETABLES FOR GREEN SMOOTHIES

This may sound strange as the whole point of green smoothies is seemingly to get large amounts of raw food. However, cooking vegetables and eating them either as a soup from your NutriBullet or as part of a smoothie is extremely healthful, particularly in winter when having warm food is, and feels, more nourishing for the body. Although some vitamins may be lost in cooking, minerals are unleashed from the fibers that are softened. Certain plant enzymes are lost as well, but these are not the enzymes necessary for digestion. It is equally important to get daily doses of both cooked and raw vegetables and perhaps less fruit which can be high in sugar.

My advice on this is to alternate your smoothies between raw and cooked or mix cooked and raw vegetables in your smoothies. This ensures you are getting all the available vitamins and minerals in today's vegetables. Just cook your vegetables until soft and pop in the NutriBullet. Limit the amount of water, and if you use onions and carrots, you can avoid fruit altogether sometimes to get a truly warming winter smoothie.

THE RECIPES

Simply Green and Smooth Recipes

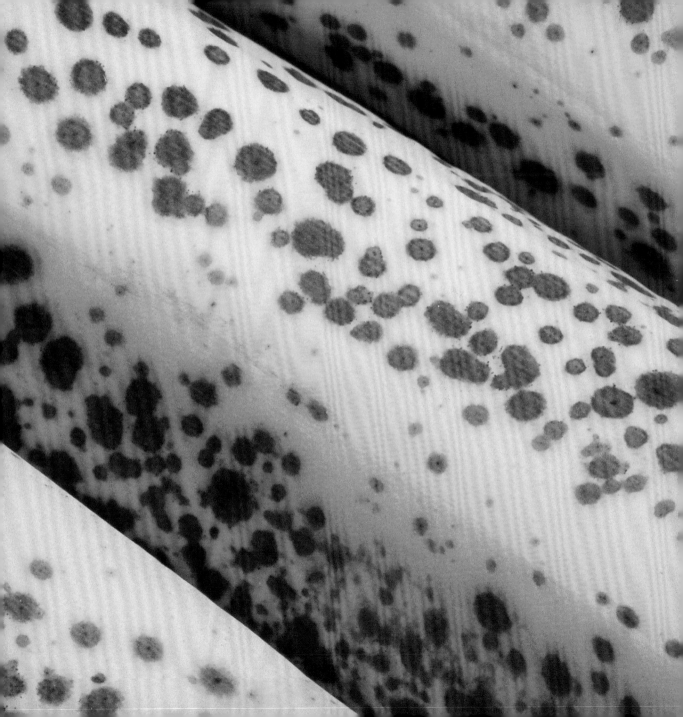

BLUE BANANA GREEN SMOOTHIE

1   FROZEN BANANA (RIPE)
A HANDFUL OF BLUEBERRIES
1   INCH OF CUCUMBER
A HANDFUL OF BABY SPINACH
1   TSP OR LESS OF HONEY
ICE
ALMOND MILK

OPTIONAL EXTRAS:
A HANDFUL OF WATERCRESS

1. Just throw all ingredients into the blender and starting low, blend well. Add a couple of ice cubes and turn up the blender.

2. Your smoothie will be crunchier if you are using almonds and water instead of almond milk.

NUTRITION:
HIGH IN B VITAMINS, VITAMIN A, VITAMIN C,
VITAMIN D, MANGANESE, FOLATE, CALCIUM,
AND POTASSIUM.

CACAO GREEN SMOOTHIE

1   FROZEN BANANA
HALF AN APPLE
1   TSP ORGANIC CACAO POWDER
1   HANDFUL OF BABY SPINACH
1   HEAPED TSP OF FLAX SEED

OPTIONAL EXTRAS:
1 TSP CACAO NIBS (WILL BE A LITTLE CRUNCHY)
A FEW SCRAPES OF A VANILLA POD OR A DASH
        OF VANILLA EXTRACT (SUGAR-FREE)

1. Blend all ingredients. This smoothie might be a little thin for your liking so if you want it thicker without adding any more ingredients, add some ice and blend. Otherwise, add an avocado.

NUTRITION:
HIGH IN VITAMIN B6, VITAMIN A, VITAMIN C,
        MANGANESE, MAGNESIUM, AND FOLATE.

BERRY & MELON GREEN SMOOTHIE

1   HANDFUL OF RASPBERRIES

A FEW CHUNKS OF CANTALOUPE MELON

1   BANANA

1   HANDFUL OF SPRING GREENS

WATER

OPTIONAL EXTRAS:

A HANDFUL OF SPROUTED BROCCOLI OR
      ALFALFA SEEDS

1. Put all the ingredients into the blender and starting low, work your way up to a high speed to really smooth out the spinach leaves.

NUTRITION:
HIGH IN VITAMIN B6, VITAMIN A , VITAMIN C, AND
      MANGANESE.

PINEAPPLE DETOX GREEN SMOOTHIE

A LITTLE GRATING OF GINGER
1   CUP OF PINEAPPLE
1   AVOCADO
1   INCH OF CUCUMBER
SEVERAL LEAVES OF ROMAINE LETTUCE
WATER

OPTIONAL EXTRAS:
SOME CELERY FOR FURTHER DETOXING
A HANDFUL OF RAW NUTS OR SEEDS

1. Start by blending the cucumber and pineapple with a little water. Then add the rest of the ingredients and speed up the blender to make smooth.

NUTRITION:
HIGH IN VITAMIN B6, VITAMIN A, VITAMIN C, COPPER, FOLATE, MANGANESE, THIAMIN, AND PANTOTHENIC ACID.

ZINGY SPRING GREEN SMOOTHIE

½ SQUEEZED LEMON
2 HANDFULS OF KALE OR SPINACH
½ APPLE
½ FROZEN BANANA
½ AVOCADO
1 TBSP OF CHIA SEEDS
WATER
ICE

1. Blend all ingredients apart from ice until smooth—then add the ice and smooth it up.

NUTRITION:
HIGH IN VITAMIN B6, VITAMIN C, CALCIUM, FOLATE,
    COPPER, PANTOTHENIC ACID, AND MANGANESE.

BERRY ROCKET GREEN SMOOTHIE

1   FROZEN BANANA
APPROX 3 STRAWBERRIES
APPROX 3 BLACKBERRIES
1   HANDFUL OF ROCKET OR ARUGULA
    LETTUCE
COCONUT MILK

1. Put all the ingredients in blender and smooth it.

NUTRITION:
HIGH IN IRON, VITAMIN A, VITAMIN B6, VITAMIN C,
COPPER, FOLATE, MAGNESIUM, MANGANESE,
PHOSPHORUS, NIACIN, THIAMIN, AND ZINC.

PEAR DELICIOUS GREEN SMOOTHIE

1   PEAR
½   AVOCADO
1   HANDFUL OF LAMB'S LETTUCE
1   HANDFUL OF CORIANDER OR CILANTRO
WATER
A LITTLE HONEY IF EXTRA SWEETNESS IS
     NEEDED
1   TSP OF MACA (OPTIONAL)

1. Blend all ingredients with ice until smooth. Taste and if your pears were not the really sweet kind, add a little honey.

NUTRITION:
HIGH IN VITAMIN A, POTASSIUM, VITAMIN B6, VITAMIN C, VITAMIN E, COPPER, FOLATE, MANGANESE, PANTOTHENIC ACID, NIACIN, AND RIBOFLAVIN.

QUICK GREEN SMOOTHIE

1   HANDFUL OF SPINACH
1   SMALL HANDFUL OF PARSLEY
1   FROZEN BANANA
½   PAPAYA (SEEDS REMOVED)
A COUPLE ICE CUBES
WATER

1. Mix all ingredients in a blender until smooth. The parsley tastes quite strong, so add more banana if you are not used to it or make with just a sprig or two.

NUTRITION:
HIGH IN POTASSIUM, IRON, VITAMIN A, VITAMIN B6, VITAMIN C, VITAMIN E, FOLATE, MAGNESIUM, AND MANGANESE.

QUICK ORANGE BREAKFAST GREEN SMOOTHIE

A HANDFUL OF LARGE SWISS CHARD LEAVES
   OR LETTUCE LEAVES
½ WHOLE ORANGES WITHOUT SEEDS AND
   PEEL
½ A GRAPEFRUIT WITHOUT SEEDS AND PEEL
½ AVOCADO
½ BANANA
ICE CUBES
WATER
OPTIONAL—A SPRINKLE OF OATS AND 1 TBSP
   OF VANILLA RICE PROTEIN POWDER

1. Throw in all ingredients and blend—then rush out the door!

NUTRITION:
HIGH IN POTASSIUM, IRON, VITAMIN A, VITAMIN
   B6, VITAMIN C, VITAMIN E, CALCIUM, COPPER,
   FOLATE, MAGNESIUM, MANGANESE, NIACIN,
   PANTOTHENIC ACID, RIBOFLAVIN, SELENIUM,
   THIAMIN, AND ZINC.

ORANGE & GO GREEN SMOOTHIE

1   ORANGE
1   AVOCADO
1   HANDFUL OF SPINACH
ALMOND MILK

OPTIONAL EXTRAS:
SOME LETTUCE AND CUCUMBER

1. Blend all together and go!

NUTRITION:
HIGH IN POTASSIUM, VITAMIN A, VITAMIN B6,
    VITAMIN C, VITAMIN D, CALCIUM, COPPER,
    FOLATE, MAGNESIUM, MANGANESE, NIACIN,
     PANTOTHENIC ACID, RIBOFLAVIN, AND THIAMINE.

CHOCO PASSION GREEN SMOOTHIE

1   FROZEN BANANA
1   HANDFUL SPINACH
1   PASSION FRUIT (THE INSIDES)
2   CHUNKS OF DARK CHOCOLATE OR 1 TSP OF
    COCOA POWDER
ALMOND MILK

1. Mix all ingredients in a blender.

NUTRITION:
HIGH IN IRON, POTASSIUM, VITAMIN A, VITAMIN
    B6, VITAMIN C, VITAMIN D, CALCIUM, COPPER,
    FOLATE, MAGNESIUM, MANGANESE, AND
        PHOSPHORUS.

SWEET GREEN SMOOTHIE

1   HANDFUL OF KALE
½   PEAR
½   BANANA
SEVERAL DATES
WATER
ICE

1. Blend everything together. Add a teaspoon of honey for an even sweeter taste.

NUTRITION:
HIGH IN POTASSIUM, VITAMIN A, VITAMIN B6,
VITAMIN C, CALCIUM, COPPER, MAGNESIUM,
MANGANESE, AND THIAMINE.

STRAWBERRY & MELON DELIGHT GREEN SMOOTHIE

1   CUP OF SWISS CHARD
1   CUP OF WATERMELON
1   INCH OF CUCUMBER
1   AVOCADO
1   TSP OF CHIA SEED OR MORE
1   SQUEEZE OF LEMON
1 OR 2 CUPS OF WATER
ICE

1. Mix all ingredients apart from the ice. Blend it well and then add the ice to cool it.

NUTRITION:
HIGH IN POTASSIUM, VITAMIN A, VITAMIN B6, VITAMIN C, COPPER, FOLATE, MAGNESIUM, MANGANESE, NIACIN, PANTOTHENIC ACID, AND THIAMINE.

TROPICAL GREEN SMOOTHIE

½ CUP OF PINEAPPLE CHUNKS
½ CUP OF MANGO
1 HANDFUL OF SPINACH
SOME COCONUT MILK, COCONUT WATER, OR
      SOME COCONUT CREAM
WATER
ICE

1. Mix ingredients in a blender until smooth. Add ice at the end. Taste and add more of either coconut or water depending on your preference.

NUTRITION:
HIGH IN POTASSIUM, VITAMIN A, VITAMIN
      B6, VITAMIN C, VITAMIN E, FOLATE, AND
          MANGANESE.

WAKE UP GREEN SMOOTHIE

1   CUP OF SPINACH
2–3 CHUNKS OF CELERY
A CHUNK OF CUCUMBER
1   FROZEN BANANA
HANDFUL OF RASPBERRIES
½–1 AVOCADO
SEVERAL MELON CHUNKS
WATER

1. Combine all ingredients and mix until smooth.

NUTRITION:
HIGH IN IRON, POTASSIUM, VITAMIN A, VITAMIN
    B6, VITAMIN C, COPPER, FOLATE, MAGNESIUM,
    MANGANESE, NIACIN, PANTOTHENIC ACID,
        RIBOFLAVIN, AND THIAMINE.

FRUITY POWER GREEN SMOOTHIE

1   CUP OF SWISS CHARD OR KALE

A FEW ARUGULA (ROCKET) LEAVES

½   KIWI

½   BANANA

1   PEACH (PITTED)

1   TSP OF WHEATGRASS OR SUPRFOOD SUCH
    AS DR. SCHULZE'S SUPERFOOD

1–2 CUPS OF WATER

1. Blend all ingredients together until smooth.

NUTRITION:
HIGH IN POTASSIUM, VITAMIN A, VITAMIN B6,
    VITAMIN C, COPPER, FOLATE, MAGNESIUM, AND
        MANGANESE.

BREAKFAST FILLER GREEN SMOOTHIE

½ APPLE

½ AVOCADO

HANDFUL OF BLUEBERRIES

1 HANDFUL OF SPINACH

1 TSP OF CHOCOLATE POWDER OR A TBSP OF
   CACAO NIBS

1 TBSP OF OATS OR INSTANT OATS

WATER OR GREEN OR WHITE TEA (CHILLED)

SEVERAL ICE CUBES

1. Blend all ingredients together and then add the ice and crush.

NUTRITION:
HIGH IN IRON, POTASSIUM, VITAMIN A, VITAMIN B6,
VITAMIN C, VITAMIN E, FOLATE, MAGNESIUM,
MANGANESE, PANTOTHENIC ACID, NIACIN,
PHOSPHORUS, RIBOFLAVIN, THIAMINE, AND ZINC.

LUNCHTIME BOOSTER GREEN SMOOTHIE

1 LARGE SLICE OF PINEAPPLE
2 LEAVES OF ROMAINE LETTUCE
½ AVOCADO
SOME SPINACH LEAVES
1 SMALL FROZEN BANANA
1 TBSP OF MILLED FLAX SEED OR CHIA SEED
1 TSP OF MACA ROOT
WATER

1. Blend all ingredients together until smooth. Add more banana for a thicker, sweeter smoothie.

NUTRITION:
HIGH IN POTASSIUM, VITAMIN A, VITAMIN B6,
VITAMIN C, FOLATE, MAGNESIUM, MANGANESE,
PANTOTHENIC ACID, AND RIBOFLAVIN.

GREEN SNACK SMOOTHIE

A LARGE HANDFUL OF LAMB'S LETTUCE
    LEAVES
APPROX 1 INCH OF CUCUMBER
A SMALL HANDFUL OF CORIANDER (CILANTRO)
    OR DANDELION LEAVES
½ AVOCADO
½ BANANA
1 HANDFUL OF BLUEBERRIES
SOME WATERMELON
WATER
ICE

1. Blend all ingredients until smooth.

NUTRITION:
HIGH IN POTASSIUM, VITAMIN C, MANGANESE,
    PANTOTHENIC ACID, AND THIAMINE.

BLACKBERRY & DATE GREEN SMOOTHIE

1   AVOCADO
A SLICE OF PINEAPPLE
A HANDFUL OF MIXED LETTUCE LEAVES
SOME BLACKBERRIES
1   TBSP FLAX SEED
1   INCH OF CUCUMBER
1   DATE
ALMOND MILK
ICE
A LITTLE HONEY (OPTIONAL)

1. Put all ingredients apart from the water in the blender and smooth it. Taste the smoothie and see if you need to add water to make it more runny or more almond milk if you like the taste.

NUTRITION:
HIGH IN POTASSIUM, VITAMIN A, VITAMIN B6, VITAMIN C, VITAMIN D, VITAMIN E, CALCIUM, COPPER, FOLATE, MAGNESIUM, MANGANESE, NIACIN, PANTOTHENIC ACID, PHOSPHORUS, AND RIBOFLAVIN.

ORANGE & PLUM GREEN SMOOTHIE

½ ORANGE
1 PLUM
½ AVOCADO
1 HANDFUL OF KALE
1 MINT LEAF
WATER
ICE CUBES

1. Blend all ingredients in the blender adding the ice as the last step.

NUTRITION:
HIGH IN IRON, POTASSIUM, VITAMIN A, VITAMIN B6,
VITAMIN C, VITAMIN D, VITAMIN E, CALCIUM,
COPPER, FOLATE, MAGNESIUM, MANGANESE,
NIACIN, PANTOTHENIC ACID, PHOSPHORUS, AND
RIBOFLAVIN.

BERRY & CABBAGE GREEN SMOOTHIE

1   HANDFUL OF STRAWBERRIES
1   HANDFUL OF CABBAGE—GREEN OR RED
    (RED MAKES A NICE BRIGHT SMOOTHIE)
1   BANANA
1   SMALL HANDFUL OF ALFALFA SPROUTS OR
    BEAN SPROUTS
½   AVOCADO
WATER

1. Blend all together and add some ice to keep it refreshing.

If you are worried about bloating and gas, you can juice the cabbage instead, which may help.

NUTRITION:
HIGH IN POTASSIUM, VITAMIN A, VITAMIN B6,
    VITAMIN C, VITAMIN D, VITAMIN E, CALCIUM,
    COPPER, FOLATE, MAGNESIUM, MANGANESE,
    NIACIN, PANTOTHENIC ACID, PHOSPHORUS, AND
    RIBOFLAVIN.

CHERRY TOP GREEN SMOOTHIE

1   CUP OF RED CHERRIES (PITTED)
1   HANDFUL OF BLUEBERRIES
1   FROZEN BANANA
1   HANDFUL OF BABY SPINACH OR CHARD
1   TBSP OF VANILLA RICE PROTEIN POWDER
    OR OTHER VANILLA PROTEIN POWDER
WATER

1. Add all ingredients into a blender and mix until smooth. You can try this with hemp or almond milk instead of water. I suggest you de-seed the cherries beforehand and freeze them—that way you can make your smoothie quickly when you want.

NUTRITION:
DEPENDS ON THE PROTEIN POWDER INGREDIENTS.
HIGH IN POTASSIUM, VITAMIN A, VITAMIN B6,
     VITAMIN C, VITAMIN D, VITAMIN E, CALCIUM,
     COPPER, FOLATE, MAGNESIUM, MANGANESE,
     NIACIN, PANTOTHENIC ACID, PHOSPHORUS, AND
     RIBOFLAVIN.

MANGO MINT GREEN SMOOTHIE

½ MANGO
1   INCH OF CUCUMBER
SEVERAL SLICES OF FROZEN BANANA
½ APPLE
A HANDFUL OF LAMBS LETTUCE AND
     WATERCRESS OR SPINACH
1   FRESH MINT LEAF
WATER
ICE

1. Blend all ingredients together until smooth. Add some ice to make it more refreshing.

NUTRITION:
HIGH IN POTASSIUM, VITAMIN A, VITAMIN B6,
     VITAMIN C, VITAMIN D, VITAMIN E, CALCIUM,
     COPPER, FOLATE, MAGNESIUM, MANGANESE,
     NIACIN, PANTOTHENIC ACID, PHOSPHORUS, AND
         RIBOFLAVIN.

MINTY BERRY GREEN SMOOTHIE

1   HANDFUL OF FROZEN RASPBERRIES
1   HANDFUL OF STRAWBERRIES
FROZEN CHUNKS OF BANANA
2   MINT LEAVES
1   HANDFUL OF GREENS OF CHOICE OR
     MUSTARD GREENS
BRAZIL NUTS

1. Blend all ingredients together and add 1 mint leaf and taste before adding another.

NUTRITION:
HIGH IN IRON, POTASSIUM, VITAMIN A, VITAMIN B6, VITAMIN C, VITAMIN D, VITAMIN E, CALCIUM, COPPER, FOLATE, MAGNESIUM, MANGANESE, NIACIN, PANTOTHENIC ACID, PHOSPHORUS, AND RIBOFLAVIN.

WATERMELON GREEN SMOOTHIE

SEVERAL CHUNKS OF WATERMELON

½   ORANGE

½   BANANA

2   KALE LEAVES OR SOME DANDELION LEAVES

A SQUEEZE OF LEMON OR LIME

WATER

ICE

OPTIONAL HALF AN AVOCADO

OPTIONAL—A HANDFUL OF STRAWBERRIES

1. You can juice the orange or cut it up and put it in blender along with the rest of the ingredients. Blend until smooth.

NUTRITION:
HIGH IN IRON, POTASSIUM, VITAMIN A, VITAMIN B6, VITAMIN C, VITAMIN D, VITAMIN E, CALCIUM, COPPER, FOLATE, MAGNESIUM, MANGANESE, NIACIN, PANTOTHENIC ACID, PHOSPHORUS, AND RIBOFLAVIN.

APPLE & CUCUMBER DETOX GREEN SMOOTHIE

1   APPLE
2   CHUNKS OF CUCUMBER
1   AVOCADO
A COUPLE OF SPRIGS OF PARSLEY
1   TSP OF HONEY

1. Mix all in a blender and add some ice for coolness. Parsley has a strong taste, so you may have to add only a small amount according to taste.

NUTRITION:
HIGH IN POTASSIUM, VITAMIN A, VITAMIN B6, VITAMIN C, COPPER, FOLATE, MAGNESIUM, MANGANESE, NIACIN, AND PANTOTHENIC ACID.

MINT CHOC CHIP GREEN SMOOTHIE

3   MINT LEAVES

1   AVOCADO

1   TSP OF ORGANIC COCOA POWDER

1   TSP OF CACAO NIBS

1   HANDFUL OF SPINACH LEAVES

1   TSP OF VANILLA EXTRACT OR ½ A VANILLA
    POD (INSIDES SCRAPED OUT)

COCONUT MILK OR COCONUT WATER OR
    ALMOND MILK

1. Add all ingredients to a blender and mix. If you are using a vanilla pod, add this last.

NUTRITION:
HIGH IN IRON, POTASSIUM, VITAMIN A, VITAMIN
    B6, VITAMIN C, COPPER, FOLATE, MAGNESIUM,
    MANGANESE, NIACIN, PANTOTHENIC ACID, AND
        PHOSPHORUS.

PARSLEY & BLUEBERRY DETOX GREEN SMOOTHIE

1 CUP OF PARSLEY APPROX.
2 CUPS OF BLUEBERRIES
1 BANANA
WATER
SEVERAL ICE CUBES
OPTIONAL—SOME MANGO

1. Mix all ingredients together in the blender.

NUTRITION:
HIGH IN IRON, POTASSIUM, VITAMIN A, VITAMIN B6,
VITAMIN C, VITAMIN E, FOLATE, MAGNESIUM,
MANGANESE, THIAMINE, AND RIBOFLAVIN.

TROPICAL SWEET GREEN SMOOTHIE

½ BANANA

A FEW CHUNKS OF PINEAPPLE

A FEW CHUNKS OF MANGO

¼ CUP OF COCONUT CREAM PLUS WATER
    OR COCONUT MILK

1   HANDFUL OF KALE LEAVES

ADDITIONAL WATER IF NECESSARY

1. Add all ingredients to blender and blend until smooth. Test the thickness and add more water if necessary.

NUTRITION:
HIGH IN POTASSIUM, VITAMIN A, VITAMIN B6,
    VITAMIN C, VITAMIN E, CALCIUM, COPPER, AND
        MANGANESE.

BREAKFAST TREAT GREEN SMOOTHIE

½   CUP OF OATMEAL OR OATS

1   BANANA

2   STRAWBERRIES

1–2 CUPS OF MILK OF CHOICE

1   HANDFUL OF SPINACH, COLLARD GREENS,
    OR OTHER GREENS OF CHOICE

EXTRA WATER IF LIMITING THE MILK CONTENT

1. Blend all ingredients until smooth.

NUTRITION:

HIGH IN IRON, POTASSIUM, VITAMIN A, B VITAMINS,
    VITAMIN C, VITAMIN D, CALCIUM, COPPER,
    FOLATE, MAGNESIUM, MANGANESE, NIACIN,
    PANTOTHENIC ACID, SELENIUM, ZINC, THIAMINE,
    PHOSPHORUS, AND RIBOFLAVIN.

CINNAMON TREAT GREEN SMOOTHIE

1   SMALL FROZEN BANANA
1   SMALL CARROT
1   SMALL APPLE
1   TSP OF CINNAMON
1   HANDFUL OF BABY SPINACH
WATER
ICE
A LITTLE HONEY

1. Blend all ingredients together until smooth.

NUTRITION:
HIGH IN POTASSIUM, VITAMIN A, VITAMIN B6,
VITAMIN C, FOLATE, AND MANGANESE.

TOMATO CREAM GREEN SMOOTHIE

2 MEDIUM TOMATOES
SEVERAL CHUNKS OF WATERMELON
½ AVOCADO
A HANDFUL OF CILANTRO OR CORIANDER
1–2 INCHES OF CELERY
A SQUEEZE OF LEMON
WATER
ICE

1. Blend all ingredients until smooth.

NUTRITION:
HIGH IN POTASSIUM, VITAMIN A, VITAMIN B6,
VITAMIN C, FOLATE, MANGANESE, AND
PANTOTHENIC ACID.

DANDELION & APPLE GREEN SMOOTHIE

2 SQUEEZES OF LEMON

1 BUNCH OF DANDELION GREENS OR GREENS
   OF CHOICE

1 APPLE

1 BANANA

1 TBSP OF MILLED CHIA SEED

WATER

OPTIONAL—CASHEW OR BRAZIL NUTS

1. Put in all the ingredients into the blender and blend—add some ice to make it refreshing.

NUTRITION:
HIGH IN POTASSIUM, VITAMIN A, VITAMIN B6,
VITAMIN C, FOLATE, AND MANGANESE.

BLACKBERRY BURST GREEN SMOOTHIE

1   LARGE ROMAINE LETTUCE LEAF
½   ORANGE (DE-SEEDED)
1   CUP OF BLACKBERRIES
A HANDFUL OF SPINACH OR KALE
SOME ZEST OF AN ORANGE (GRATED PEEL)
FROZEN BANANA CHUNKS
WATER

1. Mix all ingredients in a blender until smooth.

NUTRITION:
HIGH IN POTASSIUM, VITAMIN A, VITAMIN B6,
VITAMIN C, CALCIUM, COPPER, FOLATE,
MAGNESIUM, AND MANGANESE.

BLACKBERRY BLUE GREEN SMOOTHIE

1   HANDFUL OF SWISS CHARD
1   CUP OF BLUEBERRIES
1   CUP OF BLACKBERRIES
1   FROZEN BANANA
1   CUP OF WATER

1. Mix all ingredients in a blender until smooth.

NUTRITION:
HIGH IN POTASSIUM, VITAMIN A, VITAMIN B6,
        VITAMIN C, FOLATE, AND MANGANESE.

CHOCO PEACH GREEN SMOOTHIE

1   BANANA
1   PEACH (PITTED)
A HANDFUL OF RASPBERRIES
1   HANDFUL SPINACH
2   TSP CACAO
1   TSP MACA
WATER

1. Blend all ingredients until smooth.

NUTRITION:
HIGH IN POTASSIUM, VITAMIN A, VITAMIN B6,
VITAMIN C, COPPER, FOLATE, MAGNESIUM,
MANGANESE, NIACIN, AND RIBOFLAVIN.

BERRY BASIL GREEN SMOOTHIE

2   CUPS OF FROZEN MIXED BERRIES
A SMALL HANDFUL OF BASIL LEAVES
1   TBSP OF COCONUT CREAM
(OR YOU CAN JUST USE 1 CUP OF COCONUT
    MILK OR WATER)
1   TBSP OF FLAX SEED OR PUMPKIN SEED
WATER

1. Put all ingredients into a blender and smooth it.

NUTRITION:
HIGH IN POTASSIUM, VITAMIN C, AND MANGANESE.

BLACKBERRY & SEED GREEN SMOOTHIE

1   FROZEN BANANA
1   HANDFUL OF BLACKBERRIES
1   HANDFUL OF BABY SPINACH LEAVES
A SPRINKLE OF SEEDS OF CHOICE
1   TBSP OF VANILLA RICE PROTEIN (OR OTHER
    VANILLA-FLAVORED PROTEIN POWDER)
OAT MILK OR OTHER NON-DAIRY UNSWEETENED
    MILK ALTERNATIVE

1. Blend all together until smooth. If using pumpkin seeds, remember to soak them overnight to release their enzymes.

NUTRITION:
HIGH IN POTASSIUM, VITAMIN A, VITAMIN B6,
    VITAMIN C, VITAMIN D, VITAMIN E, CALCIUM,
    FOLATE, AND MANGANESE.

JUICE IT, SMOOTH IT RECIPES

HOT GREEN SMOOTHIE

1   CUP CARROT JUICE
½   CUP OF CELERY JUICE
½   CUP OF CUCUMBER JUICE
1   TSP HOT SAUCE
1   TSP LEMON JUICE
1   HANDFUL OF SPINACH LEAVES
SMALL HANDFUL OF PARSLEY LEAVES
ICE CUBES

1. Juice about 3 or 4 large carrots, a stick of celery, and half a cucumber.

2. Pour into the blender.

3. Add the rest of the ingredients and blend until creamy. Add an avocado for a more creamy texture.

NUTRITION:
HIGH IN IRON, POTASSIUM, VITAMIN A, VITAMIN C,
FOLATE, AND MANGANESE.

POMEGRANATE GREEN SMOOTHIE

1   CUP OF BLUEBERRIES
A FEW DRIED GOJI BERRIES
½   CUP FRESH POMEGRANATE JUICE (JUICE
     FROM 2 POMEGRANATES)
FROZEN BANANA CHUNKS
1   HANDFUL OF LAMB'S LETTUCE
WATER

1.   Juice the pomegranates.

2.   Blend with the other ingredients.

NUTRITION:
HIGH IN POTASSIUM, VITAMIN A, VITAMIN B6,
          VITAMIN C, FOLATE, AND MANGANESE.

MORNING WAKE UP GREEN SMOOTHIE

HALF A CUP OF CUCUMBER JUICE (ABOUT HALF
    A CUCUMBER)
1   HANDFUL OF SPINACH OR KALE
½   AVOCADO
1   TBSP OF RICE PROTEIN POWDER (OR OTHER)
1   HANDFUL OF RASPBERRIES
WATER
1–2 TSP MACA POWDER

1. Juice the cucumber then add to the blender. Fill with other ingredients plus water and blend until smooth.

NUTRITION:
HIGH IN POTASSIUM, VITAMIN A, VITAMIN B6,
VITAMIN C, FOLATE, MAGNESIUM, MANGANESE,
NIACIN, PANTOTHENIC ACID, AND RIBOFLAVIN.

LUNCHTIME SURVIVAL GREEN SMOOTHIE

JUICE OF 2–3 FLORETS OF BROCCOLI (HALF A
    LARGE HEAD)
1 OR 2 STICKS WORTH OF CELERY JUICE
SEVERAL CHUNKS PINEAPPLE
1   AVOCADO
FROZEN BANANA CHUNKS
A FEW STRAWBERRIES
HANDFUL OF SPINACH LEAVES
ICE CUBES
WATER

1. Juice the broccoli and celery and add to blender. Add the other ingredients and smooth it.

NUTRITION:
HIGH IN POTASSIUM, VITAMIN A, VITAMIN B6,
    VITAMIN C, COPPER, FOLATE, MAGNESIUM,
    MANGANESE, NIACIN, PANTOTHENIC ACID,
    THIAMINE, AND RIBOFLAVIN.

CHOCOLATE BLUEBERRY GREEN SMOOTHIE

1 TBSP OF CACAO NIBS OR ORGANIC DARK
  CHOCOLATE POWDER
½ CUP OF CARROT JUICE
1 FROZEN BANANA
1 CUP OF BLUEBERRIES
1 HANDFUL OF SPINACH LEAVES
WATER

1. Juice about 2 or 3 carrots. Blend with all the other ingredients until smooth.

2. Add some ice to cool it.

NUTRITION:
HIGH IN POTASSIUM, VITAMIN A, VITAMIN B6,
    VITAMIN C, VITAMIN E, FOLATE, MANGANESE,
       AND RIBOFLAVIN.

BLACKBERRY & APPLE CRUNCH GREEN SMOOTHIE

1   HANDFUL OF BLACKBERRIES
JUICE OF 1 APPLE
1   SMALL AVOCADO
1   HANDFUL OF ROMAINE LETTUCE
HANDFUL OF ALMONDS AND 2 BRAZIL NUTS
WATER
ICE CUBES

1. Juice the cucumber and apple. Add to blender with other ingredients and smooth it—add the ice last and blend again. The almonds may blend down until smooth, otherwise you will have a slightly crunchy smoothie!

NUTRITION:
HIGH IN POTASSIUM, VITAMIN A, VITAMIN B6,
    VITAMIN C, VITAMIN E, COPPER, FOLATE,
    MAGNESIUM, MANGANESE, NIACIN,
    PANTOTHENIC ACID, PHOSPHORUS, AND
        RIBOFLAVIN.

BROCCOLI BOOST GREEN SMOOTHIE

2–3 BROCCOLI FLORETS—JUICED
1   PEAR
1   APPLE
1   AVOCADO
WATER
ICE CUBES

1. Juice the broccoli and add to the blender. Mix all the other ingredients together in the blender and smooth with the ice.

NUTRITION:
HIGH IN POTASSIUM, VITAMIN B6, VITAMIN C,
    VITAMIN E, COPPER, FOLATE, MANGANESE, AND
        PANTOTHENIC ACID.

PASSION FRUIT EXPERIENCE GREEN SMOOTHIE

2   PASSION FRUIT INSIDES
A FEW STRAWBERRIES
2–3 FROZEN MANGO CHUNKS
1   HANDFUL OF CORIANDER OR CILANTRO
THE JUICE OF A SMALL CUCUMBER
WATER AS NEEDED
ICE

1. Juice the cucumber and add to blender with remaining ingredients.

2. Add a sprig of mint for garnish.

3. Add a squeeze of lime juice.

NUTRITION:
HIGH IN POTASSIUM, VITAMIN A, VITAMIN C, COPPER,
FOLATE, AND MANGANESE.

APPLE & PEAR POWER GREEN SMOOTHIE

JUICE OF 1 APPLE
JUICE OF 1 PEAR
1   AVOCADO
2   HANDFULS OF BABY SPINACH
1   TSP OF GREEN SUPERFOOD POWDER OF
    CHOICE
ADD WATER AS NEEDED

1. Juice the apple and pear. Add to the blender with the rest of the ingredients and smooth it.

NUTRITION:
HIGH IN POTASSIUM, VITAMIN A, VITAMIN B6,
    VITAMIN C, FOLATE, MANGANESE, PANTOTHENIC
        ACID, AND RIBOFLAVIN.

APPLE & LEMON GREEN SMOOTHIE

1–2 HANDFULS OF SPRING GREENS
SQUEEZE FROM HALF A LEMON
1   APPLE-JUICED
½   AVOCADO
½   BANANA
WATER
ICE

1. Juice the apples and lemon (or you can just squeeze).

2. Blend all ingredients together in blender until smooth.

NUTRITION:
HIGH IN POTASSIUM, VITAMIN B6, VITAMIN C, AND
        FOLATE.

KIWI PARADISE GREEN SMOOTHIE

JUICE OF 1 APPLE

1 KIWI FRUIT

1 HANDFUL OF SWISS CHARD

½ AN AVOCADO

A SQUEEZE OF LIME

WATER

ICE

2 MINT LEAVES (OPTIONAL)

OPTIONAL—CASHEW NUTS

1. Juice the apple and add to the blender. Add all other ingredients and blend.

NUTRITION:
HIGH IN POTASSIUM, VITAMIN A, VITAMIN B6,
VITAMIN C, COPPER, FOLATE, AND MANGANESE.

BEET IT GREEN SMOOTHIE

JUICE OF 1 RAW BEETROOT

½   APPLE

½   AN AVOCADO

1   HANDFUL OF LETTUCE OF CHOICE

1   SQUEEZE OF LEMON

1   TSP OF CACAO NIBS

1   TSP OF MILLED CHIA SEEDS

WATER

ICE

1. Juice the beetroot and add to the blender. Add the other ingredients to the blender and smooth with the ice.

NUTRITION:
HIGH IN POTASSIUM, VITAMIN C, FOLATE, AND
        MANGANESE.

FENNEL FANTASTIC GREEN SMOOTHIE

JUICE OF ½ A FENNEL BULB
JUICE OF AN ORANGE
JUICE OF ½ A LIME
½   AN AVOCADO
½   A BANANA
2 OR 3 MINT LEAVES
1   CUP OF WATER
ICE

1. Juice the fennel and squeeze the lime and orange and add to the blender and mix with the other ingredients.

NUTRITION:
HIGH IN POTASSIUM, VITAMIN B6, VITAMIN C, AND
        FOLATE.

BRUSSELS SPROUT GREEN SMOOTHIE

JUICE OF 3 BRUSSELS SPROUTS
JUICE OF ½ CUCUMBER
JUICE OF 1 APPLE
1   AVOCADO
A SQUEEZE OF LEMON
SOME SPINACH AS DESIRED
WATER AS NEEDED

1. Juice the apples and brussels sprouts. Add to the blender with the other ingredients. Smooth it.

NUTRITION:
HIGH IN POTASSIUM, VITAMIN B6, VITAMIN C, FOLATE, AND PANTOTHENIC ACID.

Green Smoothie Joy

QUICK COLD FIX GREEN SMOOTHIE

JUICE OF 1 ORANGE (OR YOU CAN BLEND AN
    ORANGE IF YOU PREFER)

A HANDFUL OF RASPBERRIES

½ KIWI FRUIT

A LONG SQUEEZE OF LEMON

1   TSP OF GREEN BARLEY GRASS OR OTHER
    GREEN SUPERFOOD

A FEW BANANA CHUNKS

A HANDFUL OF LEAFY GREENS OF CHOICE

1   TSP OF HONEY

1. Juice the orange. Combine in blender with other ingredients.

NUTRITION:
HIGH IN POTASSIUM, VITAMIN B6, VITAMIN C,
    FOLATE, MAGNESIUM, AND MANGANESE.

BODY BOOSTING GREEN SMOOTHIE

1 SMALL JUICED RAW BEETROOT
1 JUICED CARROT
1 JUICED STICK OF CELERY
1 AVOCADO
1 HANDFUL OF BABY SPINACH LEAVES
1 HANDFUL OF BLUEBERRIES
WATER
ICE

1. Juice the beet, carrot, and celery. Add to blender with the other ingredients.

NUTRITION:
HIGH IN POTASSIUM, VITAMIN A, VITAMIN B6,
VITAMIN C, VITAMIN E, COPPER, FOLATE,
MAGNESIUM, MANGANESE, NIACIN,
PANTOTHENIC ACID, AND RIBOFLAVIN.

APPLE & CARROT GREEN SMOOTHIE

JUICE OF 1 APPLE
JUICE OF 1 CARROT
JUICE OF 1 CELERY STICK
1 AVOCADO
½ CUCUMBER
DASH OF LEMON
ICE
WATER
NUTS AS DESIRED FOR THICKNESS AND
    PROTEIN

1. Juice the apples, carrot, and celery. Add to the blender with the other ingredients. Blend with the ice.

NUTRITION:
HIGH IN POTASSIUM, VITAMIN A, VITAMIN B6,
    VITAMIN C, FOLATE, MAGNESIUM, MANGANESE,
        NIACIN, PANTOTHENIC ACID, AND RIBOFLAVIN.

Green Smoothie Joy

SOME FRUITY, SOME YOGURTY SMOOTHIES

STRAWBERRY GRAPEFRUIT DETOXIFYING SMOOTHIE

½ A GRAPEFRUIT
1 HANDFUL OF RASPBERRIES
½ BANANA
WATER
ICE
2 BRAZIL NUTS,
PLUS ANYTHING GREEN
OPTIONAL—ADD LIVE YOGURT FOR AN EVEN
    CREAMIER TEXTURE

1. Blend all ingredients until smooth. Add a little water first and then check consistency before adding the full cup.

NUTRITION:
HIGH IN POTASSIUM, VITAMIN B6, VITAMIN C,
    MANGANESE, AND RIBOFLAVIN.

APPLE & MELON SMOOTHIE

1   CUP OF HONEYDEW MELON, CUT INTO
    PIECES
½   APPLE
2   TBSP OF ORGANIC LIVE YOGURT (GREEK
    YOGURT IS NICE AND THICK)
1   TBSP LIME JUICE
1   CUP OF WATER
ICE CUBES
OPTIONAL—SPINACH LEAVES

1. Place all the ingredients into the blender and smooth it.

NUTRITION:
HIGH IN POTASSIUM, VITAMIN B6, VITAMIN C, AND
        FOLATE.

SWEET PEAR SMOOTHIE

1   PEAR (CORED)
1   BANANA
1   TSP HONEY
ALMOND MILK
ICE
HANDFUL OF ROCKET OR ARUGULA
OPTIONAL—1 TBSP FLAX SEEDS

1. Blend all together until smooth.

NUTRITION:
HIGH IN POTASSIUM, VITAMIN B6, VITAMIN C,
VITAMIN D, VITAMIN E, AND CALCIUM.

PAPAYA STRAWBERRY SMOOTHIE

1   PAPAYA, PEELED AND DICED
½   FROZEN BANANA
A FEW CHUNKS PINEAPPLE
A FEW STRAWBERRIES
 WATER
ICE
OPTIONAL—A CHUNK OF CUCUMBER
SPINACH OR LAMBS LETTUCE

1.   Blend all ingredients and then add the ice.

NUTRITION:
HIGH IN POTASSIUM, VITAMIN A, VITAMIN B6,
VITAMIN C, FOLATE, AND MANGANESE.

PASSION & MANGO SMOOTHIE

½   MANGO
1   CUP OF PINEAPPLE
1   PASSION FRUIT
FROZEN BANANA CHUNKS
WATER

1.   Smooth all the ingredients in a blender and serve with ice.

NUTRITION:
HIGH IN POTASSIUM, VITAMIN A, VITAMIN B6,
    VITAMIN C, VITAMIN E, COPPER, FOLATE,
    MAGNESIUM, MANGANESE, NIACIN, RIBOFLAVIN,
    AND NIACIN.

CHERRY BERRY SMOOTHIE

1   CUP OF CHERRIES (PITTED)
FROZEN BANANA CHUNKS
SOME RASPBERRIES
½   APPLE
WATER
ICE
OPTIONAL—DARK CHOCOLATE CHUNKS OR
    1–2 TSP OF COCOA POWDER OR CACAO NIBS
OPTIONAL—GREEN LEAVES

1. Blend all the ingredients along with the ice and a little water. Add more water if you need it.

NUTRITION:
HIGH IN POTASSIUM, VITAMIN B6, VITAMIN C, COPPER, MAGNESIUM, MANGANESE, AND RIBOFLAVIN.

POM BERRY SMOOTHIE

A HANDFUL OF STRAWBERRIES
JUICE OF 1 POMEGRANATE
1   BANANA OR AVOCADO
A HANDFUL OF RASPBERRIES
WATER OR ALMOND MILK
ICE

1. Juice the pomegranates and then place all the ingredients in the blender and mix until smooth.

NUTRITION:
HIGH IN POTASSIUM, VITAMIN B6, VITAMIN C,
VITAMIN D, VITAMIN E, CALCIUM, FOLATE,
MAGNESIUM, MANGANESE, AND RIBOFLAVIN.

COCO MANGO SMOOTHIE

½ MANGO
½ BANANA
A FEW CHUNKS OF PINEAPPLE
1   TBSP OF COCONUT CREAM OR 1 CUP OF
    COCONUT MILK
WATER
ICE

1. Just put the ingredients into the blender and whizz it!

2. Great for a quick fruit blast.

NUTRITION:
HIGH IN POTASSIUM, VITAMIN A, VITAMIN B6,
    VITAMIN C, VITAMIN D, VITAMIN E, CALCIUM,
        COPPER, MANGANESE, AND THIAMINE.

PEACH & ALMOND SMOOTHIE

2 SLICES OF PINEAPPLE
1 BANANA
A HANDFUL OF SWEET ALMONDS OR PECANS
1 PEACH, PITTED
½ AN AVOCADO
WATER
OPTIONAL—PUMPKIN OR FLAX SEEDS

1. Blend all together in the blender.

NUTRITION:
HIGH IN POTASSIUM, VITAMIN B6, VITAMIN C,
VITAMIN E, COPPER, FOLATE, MAGNESIUM,
MANGANESE, NIACIN, PANTOTHENIC ACID,
PHOSPHORUS, THIAMIN, AND RIBOFLAVIN.

BLUEBERRY NUT SMOOTHIE

1   PEACH

1   CUP OF BLUEBERRIES

2   BRAZIL NUTS OR OTHER

¼ TSP VANILLA EXTRACT

WATER

ICE

OPTIONAL—ADD SPINACH FOR THE GREEN
    NUTRITION

1. Combine all ingredients in the blender and smooth it.

NUTRITION:
HIGH IN POTASSIUM, VITAMIN C, VITAMIN E, AND
    MANGANESE.

PINEAPPLE & NECTARINE ENERGY SMOOTHIE

½ BANANA
1 NECTARINE, PEELED, PITTED, AND CUT IN CHUNKS
2 SLICES OF PINEAPPLE
WATER OR MILK
1 TBSP OF PROTEIN POWDER (VANILLA RICE PROTEIN)
ICE AS REQUIRED

1. Place all the ingredients into the blender and blend until smooth.

NUTRITION:
HIGH IN POTASSIUM, VITAMIN A, B VITAMINS, VITAMIN C, VITAMIN D, CALCIUM, COPPER, MANGANESE, NIACIN, PANTOTHENIC ACID, PHOSPHORUS, THIAMINE, AND RIBOFLAVIN.

MELON BERRY YOGURT SMOOTHIE

½ OF A CANTALOUPE MELON

1 CUP OF STRAWBERRIES

½ BANANA

1 CUP OF LIVE (HEALTHY BACTERIA INCLUDED)
   YOGURT

ADD WATER AS NEEDED

OPTIONAL—GREEN LEAVES SUCH AS LETTUCE

1. Mix all together in blender.

NUTRITION:
HIGH IN POTASSIUM, VITAMIN A, B VITAMINS, VITAMIN
C, CALCIUM, COPPER, FOLATE, MAGNESIUM,
MANGANESE, PANTOTHENIC ACID, PHOSPHORUS,
THIAMINE, ZINC, AND RIBOFLAVIN.

FILL UP AND GO GREEN SMOOTHIES

FRUITY PUNCH SMOOTHIE

1   TBSP OF PROTEIN POWDER
1   HANDFUL OF SPINACH
1   SLICE OF PINEAPPLE
SEVERAL STRAWBERRIES
A FEW BANANA CHUNKS
1   NECTARINE
1   TSP OF FLAX SEED, CHIA SEED, OR PUMPKIN
     SEEDS
WATER
ICE

1.   Blend all together and add ice for a cool smoothie.

NUTRITION:
HIGH IN POTASSIUM, VITAMIN A, VITAMIN B6,
    VITAMIN C, COPPER, FOLATE, MAGNESIUM, AND
    MANGANESE.

CHOCOLATE BOOST GREEN SMOOTHIE

1   HANDFUL OF BLUEBERRIES

1   HANDFUL OF BABY LEAF GREENS

½   BANANA

1   TSP OF RICE PROTEIN

1   TSP OF MACA

1   TSP OF CACAO POWDER, NIBS, OR ORGANIC
    DARK COCOA POWDER

ALMOND MILK OR OTHER MILK OF CHOICE, OR
    WATER

ICE

1. Blend all ingredients together and add some ice at the end.

NUTRITION:
HIGH IN POTASSIUM, VITAMIN A, VITAMIN B6,
VITAMIN C, VITAMIN D, VITAMIN E, CALCIUM,
FOLATE, AND MANGANESE.

WINTRY GREEN SMOOTHIE

1   BANANA
1   CUP OF FROZEN BERRIES
½   AN ORANGE
A HANDFUL OF SPINACH OR KALE
WATER

1. Mix all in the blender until smooth. Add water as necessary. If too sweet, add a little squeeze of lemon.

NUTRITION:
HIGH IN POTASSIUM, VITAMIN A, VITAMIN B6, VITAMIN C, COPPER, FOLATE, MAGNESIUM, MANGANESE, AND RIBOFLAVIN.

GRAPEFRUIT & PINEAPPLE DIET YOGURT SMOOTHIE

SEVERAL CHUNKS OF PINEAPPLE
1   SMALL AVOCADO
A FEW LEAVES OF LETTUCE
½   A GRAPEFRUIT
A BIG SQUEEZE OF LIME
2   TBSP PLAIN LIVE YOGURT
WATER

1. Blend all ingredients until smooth.

NUTRITION:
HIGH IN POTASSIUM, VITAMIN A, B VITAMINS,
     VITAMIN C, CALCIUM, COPPER, FOLATE,
     MAGNESIUM, MANGANESE, NIACIN,
     PANTOTHENIC ACID, PHOSPHORUS, THIAMINE,
      ZINC, AND RIBOFLAVIN.

COCOA BANANA SMOOTHIE

1   BANANA

A HANDFUL OF FROZEN BERRIES MIX

1   TBSP OF COCOA POWDER OR RAW CACAO
     POWDER

1   TSP OF GREEN SUPERFOOD

1   TSP OF MACA ROOT POWDER

COCONUT WATER OR CREAM AND ADD WATER
     (OR 1 CUP OF ALMOND MILK)

1   TSP OF MANUKA HONEY

1.   Mix all together and blend away!

NUTRITION:

HIGH IN POTASSIUM, VITAMIN B6, VITAMIN C,
     COPPER, FOLATE, MAGNESIUM, MANGANESE,
     AND RIBOFLAVIN.

STRAWBERRY CREAM GREEN SMOOTHIE

2   HANDFULS OF STRAWBERRIES

2   BANANAS

1   HANDFUL OF BABY SPINACH LEAVES

A SMALL HANDFUL OF GOJI BERRIES (SOAKED
     BEFOREHAND FOR APPROX 5 MINUTES)

1   CUP OF MILK OF CHOICE (COW'S, OAT, RICE,
     COCONUT, ETC.)

ICE

1   TSP OF VANILLA EXTRACT (OPTIONAL)

1. Blend the mixture until it is smooth. Garnish with a couple of blueberries.

NUTRITION:
HIGH IN POTASSIUM, VITAMIN A, VITAMIN B6,
    VITAMIN C, VITAMIN D, CALCIUM, COPPER,
    FOLATE, MAGNESIUM, MANGANESE,
    PANTOTHENIC ACID, PHOSPHORUS, AND
    RIBOFLAVIN.

COFFEE & ALMOND BREAKFAST SMOOTHIE

1   CUP OF COOLED BLACK COFFEE
A HANDFUL OF ALMONDS OR ½ CUP OF
    ALMOND MILK
1   BANANA
1   HANDFUL OF BLUEBERRIES
A SPRINKLE OF CINNAMON
1   HANDFUL OF SPINACH LEAVES
EXTRA WATER OR MILK
1   TSP HONEY (OPTIONAL)

1. Mix everything in a blender.

NUTRITION:
HIGH IN POTASSIUM, VITAMIN A, VITAMIN B6,
    VITAMIN C, VITAMIN E, COPPER, FOLATE,
    MAGNESIUM, MANGANESE, RIBOFLAVIN, AND
        THIAMINE.

SALAD SMOOTHIE

1   AVOCADO (OR YOU CAN USE 2 CUPS OF
    YOGURT INSTEAD)
½   CUCUMBER
1   TOMATO
A SMALL BUNCH OF CHIVES
A HANDFUL OF CILANTRO OR CORIANDER
CELERY CHUNKS
HANDFUL OF ROMAINE LETTUCE LEAVES
WATER
ICE
SALT AND PEPPER (OPTIONAL)

1. Mix all together in a blender and whizz until smooth.

NUTRITION:
HIGH IN POTASSIUM, VITAMIN A, VITAMIN B6,
    VITAMIN C, COPPER, FOLATE, MAGNESIUM,
    MANGANESE, NIACIN, PANTOTHENIC ACID,
        PHOSPHORUS, AND RIBOFLAVIN.

Green Smoothie Joy

TIME CRUNCHED SMOOTHIES

Strawberry Orange Smoothie

Make this with strawberries, a little honey, a banana, and an orange or orange juice.

Quick Blueberry Smoothie

Use blueberries, yogurt, or avocado, and banana.

Taste the Tropics Smoothie

Blend banana, mango, pineapple, kiwi, and an orange.

Berry Smoothie

Blend your frozen berries with yogurt or banana and milk (or water).

Pina Colada Smoothie

Blend pineapple, coconut cream, and water or coconut water, with banana.

Add a tablespoon of seeds with any of these

Such as sunflower, chia, etc. If you are adding unmilled seeds you may not get them to blend very well and you will have to drink your smoothie without a straw and with a definite crunch.

VERY SWEET NAUGHTY SMOOTHIES

JAM SMOOTHIE

1   CUP UNSWEETENED VANILLA YOGURT OR
    PLAIN YOGURT AND VANILLA EXTRACT
½ TO 1 BANANA
1   CUP OF RASPBERRIES
1   TBSP OF NATURALLY SWEETENED JAM
2 CUPS OF WATER

1. Blend all until smooth and creamy.

NUTRITION:
HIGH IN POTASSIUM, MAGNESIUM, B6, B12, C,
    CALCIUM, FOLATE, MANGANESE, PANTOTHENIC
        ACID, PHOSPHORUS, RIBOFLAVIN, ZINC.

CREAMY PEANUT BUTTER BERRY SMOOTHIE

½   BANANA

1   CUP OF MIXED FROZEN BERRIES

½   CUP OF CREAM

1   TBSP OF PEANUT BUTTER (UNSWEETENED)

1   TSP OF COCOA POWDER OR CACAO POWDER

2   TSP MAPLE SYRUP OR AGAVE SYRUP

WATER

1. Place the banana and strawberry chunks into the blender. Pour in the water and cream then the rest of the ingredients.

2. Blend until smooth.

NUTRITION:
HIGH IN VIT   B6, VIT C, MANGANESE, MAGNESIUM
        AND PHOSPHOROUS, RIBOFLAVIN AND ZINC.

SWEET YOGURT & WATERMELON SMOOTHIE

1   CUP OF GREEK YOGURT WITH NATURAL
    BACTERIA
1   TBSP OF HONEY
2   CUPS OF WATERMELON
WATER
½   CUCUMBER (OPTIONAL)
2   DATES OR CASHEWS OR PECANS (OPTIONAL)

1. Blend all together for a thick smoothie.

NUTRITION:
HIGH IN POTASSIUM, VITAMIN C, B-12, B-6, A,
    CALCIUM, PHOSPHOROUS, THIAMIN AND
        RIBOFLAVIN.

POMEGRANATE & STRAWBERRIES SMOOTHIE

½ CUP OF FRESH POMEGRANATE JUICE

½ BANANA

A HANDFUL OF STRAWBERRIES (OR MIXED
   FROZEN BERRIES)

1 LARGE TBSP OF CRÈME FRAICHE OR LOW-
   FAT PLAIN YOGURT

WATER

ICE

1 TSP OF HONEY (OPTIONAL)

1. Put all ingredients into blender and mix until smooth.

NUTRITION: USING LOW FAT PLAIN YOGURT
HIGH IN VITAMIN B6, C, POTASSIUM, CALCIUM,
      PHOSPHOROUS, RIBOFLAVIN.

BLUEBERRY ICE CREAM SMOOTHIE

1   CUP OF BLUEBERRIES (OR ANY CHOSEN
    BERRY) (FROZEN IS BEST)
½   A BANANA
1   CUP OF VANILLA OR CHOCOLATE ICE CREAM
1   CUP OF MILK (APPROXIMATELY)
ICE
1   TSP OF HONEY (OPTIONAL)
A SPRINKLE OR TWO OF CINNAMON (OPTIONAL)

1. Put all the ingredients in the blender, adding the milk last. Add the milk a little at time so you don't make the smoothie too thin. You can add any milk you like—almond would be a good choice.

2. Blend until smooth.

NUTRITION:
    HIGH IN VITAMIN C, D, MANGANESE CALCIUM.

CINNAMON APPLE SMOOTHIE

1 APPLE
½ BANANA
1–2 TBSPS OF GREEK YOGURT WITH NATURAL
    BACTERIA
1 TSP OF CINNAMON
1 TSP OF HONEY
ALMOND MILK (OR WATER AND A HANDFUL OF
    ALMONDS FOR A THICKER SMOOTHIE)
ICE

1. Blend all ingredients together until smooth. Add a few cubes of ice as you go and check consistency.

NUTRITION:
HIGH IN POTASSIUM, VITAMIN E, VITAMIN B-6, C,
        CALCIUM, PHOSPHOROUS AND RIBOFLAVIN.

CHOCCY GINGER BANANA SMOOTHIE

1 BANANA
SOME GRATED GINGER
SEVERAL CHUNKS OF DARK CHOCOLATE OR 1
    TBSP OF DARK COCOA POWDER (SUGAR-
    FREE)
WATER OR MILK OF CHOICE
ICE
OPTIONAL—SOME GREENS LIKE SPINACH
    WITHOUT A STRONG TASTE

1. Mix all together in a blender and enjoy.

SEEDY SMOOTHIES

Instructions for all: Simply combine and blend.

PUMPKIN PROTEIN SMOOTHIE

ADD 1 TO 2 CUPS OF PUMPKIN SEEDS
1 PEAR
½ AVOCADO
A HANDFUL OF KALE
A DATE OR TWO FOR EXTRA SWEETNESS
WATER

NUTRITION:
HIGH IN VITAMIN A, E, AND C AND A MODERATE AMOUNT OF TRACE MINERALS.

SUNFLOWER SATISFYING SMOOTHIE

2 HANDFULS OF SUNFLOWER SEEDS
1 BANANA
½ AVOCADO
SOME BERRIES OF CHOICE
1 TBSP OF FLAX SEED

A LARGE HANDFUL OF SPINACH
A SQUEEZE OF LEMON
WATER
ICE

NUTRITION:
HIGH IN VITAMIN A, E, C, B6, AND HIGH IN TRACE MINERALS.

OMEGA 3 BOOST SMOOTHIE

2 TBSP OF FLAX SEED
1 TSP OF CHIA SEED
1 AVOCADO
1 APPLE
A HANDFUL OF STRAWBERRIES OR TRY FROZEN PINEAPPLE AND MANGO CHUNKS

A COUPLE OF FLORETS OF BROCCOLI
SOME GREEN LEAVES OF CHOICE
1 DATE

NUTRITION:
HIGH IN VITAMIN A, E, C, B6, COPPER, MANGANESE, AND OTHER TRACE MINERALS.

FRUIT-FREE SMOOTHIES

MUESLI SMOOTHIE

Add 1 cup of preferred muesli. I used a nutty muesli (sugar free) from Dorset Cereals. Or you can throw in 2 tbsp each of oats, barley flakes, wheat flakes, some almonds, a couple of brazil nuts, sunflower seeds

2–3 FLORETS OF BROCCOLI OR GREEN BEANS
FILL TO MAX LINE WITH EITHER WATER OR
    ALMOND MILK OR OTHER MILK OF CHOICE

1. Blend well for a creamy smoothie.

NUTRITION:
HIGH IN IRON, MANGANESE, FOLATE, VITAMIN B12, B6 AND THIAMIN, NIACIN, AND CALCIUM PLUS A FAIR AMOUNT OF OTHER TRACE MINERALS.

VEGGIE VIRGIN SMOOTHIE

1 HANDFUL OF SPINACH
HALF A CARROT
SOME KALE
A FEW CHUNKS OF CELERY
HALF A TOMATO
¼ OR LESS OF GARLIC CLOVE

½ AVOCADO OR NUTS TO ADD THICKNESS
WATER AND ICE

NUTRITION:
HIGH IN VITAMIN A, B6, C, FOLATE, AND TRACE MINERALS SUCH AS MANGANESE.

SPICY VEG SMOOTHIE

3 ASPARAGUS STALKS
HALF A SMALL RED ONION
A HANDFUL OF CASHEW NUTS
A COUPLE OF BRAZIL NUTS
HALF A RED PEPPER
A HANDFUL OF LEAFY GREENS OF CHOICE
1 TBSP OF FLAX SEED

A LARGE SQUEEZE OF LEMON
WATER
ICE
OPTIONAL—CHILLI POWDER OR FLAKES

NUTRITION:
HIGH IN VITAMIN A, C, IRON, MAGNESIUM, MANGANESE, AND OTHER TRACE MINERALS.

VERY NUTTY SMOOTHIES

PECAN & MACADAMIA SMOOTHIE

1   HANDFUL OF PECANS
1   HANDFUL OF MACADAMIA NUTS (YOU CAN CHANGE
    THE NUTS TO WALNUTS AND ALMONDS FOR VARIETY)
1   BANANA
1   HANDFUL OF CILANTRO
1   LARGE ROMAINE LETTUCE LEAF

½   AN AVOCADO
WATER
ICE

NUTRITION:
HIGH IN VITAMIN A, C, B6, AND OTHER TRACE MINERALS.

CASHEW CREAM SMOOTHIE

2   HANDFULS OF RAW CASHEWS
3   BRAZIL NUTS
1   PASSION FRUIT
1   BANANA
1   HANDFUL OF GREENS OF CHOICE

NUTRITION:
HIGH IN VITAMIN A, C, B6, MAGNESIUM, COPPER, AND
    OTHER TRACE MINERALS.

MIXED NUT & OAT SMOOTHIE

1–2 CUPS OF MIXED NUTS
½   CUP OF OATS
1   BANANA
SOME GREEN BEANS
SOME SPINACH

A TSP OF HONEY IF DESIRED
WATER
ICE

NUTRITION:
HIGH IN VITAMIN A, C, B6, AND IRON PLUS A VARIETY OF
    TRACE MINERALS.

SPECIFIC HEALTH SMOOTHIES

ADRENAL SUPPORT SMOOTHIE

2–3 FLORETS OF BROCCOLI
1   HANDFUL OF KALE
1   AVOCADO
SEVERAL BANANA CHUNKS
HANDFUL OF CHERRIES
2–3 BRAZIL NUTS
1   HANDFUL OF PUMPKIN SEEDS
OPTIONAL EXTRA STRAWBERRIES
WATER

1. (Keep the body nice and warm if its a cold day so leave out the ice unless its a baking hot day.)

2. Optional extra—a capsule of dried cherries e.g. CherryActive emptied into the drink (excellent for immune and inflammation).

3. Or—1 tsp to 1 tbsp of maca root powder—said to help with hormonal balancing but if using for the first time with adrenal fatigue start of with half to 1 tsp of it. And always take in the morning.

4. You can leave out the fruit, add a carrot and heat the smoothie for a warm effect in a saucepan. Alternatively, cook the vegetables before putting in the NutriBullet.

NUTRITION:
NUTRITION: HIGH IN VITAMINS A AND C, FOLATE, MANGANESE, COPPER, B-6, AND OTHER TRACE MINERALS.

THYROID SUPPORT SMOOTHIE

1–2 HANDFULS OF MACADAMIA NUTS
1–2 BRAZIL NUTS
1–2 SHEETS OF PACKAGED SEAWEED
    OR 1 TSP OF GREEN SUPERFOOD POWDER
1   CUP OF BLUEBERRIES
1   CUP OF PEAS
1–2 TSP OF COCONUT OIL
1   TBSP FLAXSEED
1   HANDFUL OF SUNFLOWER SEEDS
2   TBSP OF PLAIN YOGURT
WATER

NUTRITION:
HIGH IN VITAMIN A, C, B-6, MANGANESE, THIAMIN, PHOSPHORUS, ZINC, AND OTHER TRACE MINERALS.

HEART HEALTH SMOOTHIE

½   CUP OF OATMEAL
1   CHUNK OF DARK CHOCOLATE—WITH OR WITHOUT
    SUGAR
THE FLESH OF ½ A POMEGRANATE
1   TBSP OLIVE OIL
A FEW GREEN BEANS
A COUPLE OF FLORETS OF BROCCOLI
1   HANDFUL OF FROZEN BLUEBERRIES
½   AVOCADO
WATER

NUTRITION:
HIGH IN VITAMIN C, FOLATE, MANGANESE, AND
    MOST TRACE MINERALS.

DETOX & CLEANSING SMOOTHIE

JUICE OF 1 BEET
JUICE OF ½ CARROT
JUICE OF ¼ FENNEL BULB
2   ASPARAGUS STALKS
SOME CELERY CHUNKS
1   AVOCADO
WATER
ICE IF DESIRED

NUTRITION:
HIGH IN VITAMINS A AND C, FOLATE,
    POTASSIUM, AND MANY TRACE MINERALS.

METRIC AND IMPERIAL CONVERSIONS

(These conversions are rounded for convenience)

Ingredient	Cups/Tablespoons/Teaspoons	Ounces	Grams/Milliliters
Fruit, dried	1 cup	4 ounces	120 grams
Fruits or veggies, chopped	1 cup	5 to 7 ounces	145 to 200 grams
Fruits or veggies, pureed	1 cup	8.5 ounces	245 grams
Honey, maple syrup, or corn syrup	1 tablespoon	.75 ounce	20 grams
Liquids: cream, milk, water, or juice	1 cup	8 fluid ounces	240 ml
Oats	1 cup	5.5 ounces	150 grams
Spices: cinnamon, cloves, ginger, or nutmeg (ground)	1 teaspoon	0.2 ounce	5 ml

RESOURCES

Experience Life – "Smart Juicing"

http://experiencelife.com/article/smart-juicing/

Health and wellness magazine's take on the pros and cons of juicing fruits and vegetables.

The Blender: A Williams-Sonoma Blog – "30 Days of Juicing"

http://blog.williams-sonoma.com/30-days-of-juicing/

A 30-day juicing program that works to gradually initiate new users, moving from "easy" to more unconventional juice combinations.

Raw-Foods-Diet-Center.com

http://www.raw-foods-diet-center.com/

A website that features the benefits of raw foods; listings include juicing recipes, raw foods recipes, and smoothie recipes.

All About Juicing

http://www.all-about-juicing.com/

A web guide to juicing for health, providing benefits, juicer reviews, free recipes, and more.

Juicing for Men

http://juicingformen.com/

A website that focuses on improving men's health through juicing and a more natural lifestyle.

FitDay.com – "The Risks and Benefits of Juicing"

http://www.fitday.com/fitness-articles/nutrition/the-risks-and-benefits-of-juicing.html

A health and fitness website that offers a licensed dietician's take on the pros and cons of juicing.

Raw Family

http://www.rawfamily.com/

A website/blog that focuses on green smoothies and raw foods to lead to a healthier lifestyle.

Simple Green Smoothies

http://simplegreensmoothies.com/

Informational website that provides recipes, articles on health and smoothies, and a 30-day challenge.

Healthy Blender Recipes

http://healthyblenderrecipes.com/

A website/blog that focuses on various blender recipes on everything from gluten- and dairy-free to raw foods based.

The Raw Food World

http://therawfoodworld.com/

A website and online store that features information and products that fit the raw food lifestyle.

Raw Food Life!

http://www.rawfoodlife.com

A website that provides information and articles on the science behind raw food health and other healthy living tips.

Rawmazing

http://www.rawmazing.com/why-raw/

A website that highlights the health benefits of eating raw foods, while also providing recipes, suggestions, and other resources.

Eating Well

http://www.eatingwell.com/

A website that focuses on healthier living by focusing on your diet and eating better.

MindBodyGreen

http://www.mindbodygreen.com/

A website that takes a look at total lifestyle techniques for a healthier mind and body.

Choosing Raw

http://www.choosingraw.com/

A website that focuses on making the choice to lead a vegan and raw lifestyle.

Young and Raw

http://www.youngandraw.com/

A lifestyle website that offers ideas and information to help young adults/professionals lead a raw, healthy life.

Health.com

http://www.health.com/health/

The online version of the magazine *Health*, it offers tips and articles on diets, fitness, recipes, and more to lead a healthy life.

Skyhorse Publishing

http://www.skyhorsepublishing.com/catalog/?category_id=227

Online catalog of books that provide information on healthy living, recipes, and fitness.

Live Healthy America

http://www.livehealthyamerica.org/

An online guide to leading a healthier lifestyle through nutrition and fitness.

Mayo Clinic

http://www.mayoclinic.com/health/HealthyLivingIndex/HealthyLivingIndex

A national research institution that provides online information for leading a healthy lifestyle.

Cooking Light

http://www.cookinglight.com/healthy-living/

Online extension of the *Cooking Light* magazine that helps users better prepare healthier foods.

MSN Healthy Living

http://healthyliving.msn.com/

News outlet division that focuses on providing online content to help people lead a healthy lifestyle (fitness, nutrition, disease, wellness, etc.).

Centers for Disease Control and Prevention

http://www.cdc.gov/healthyliving/

The online resource for the government department focused on the health of Americans through lifestyle changes and illness prevention.

Healthy Living: How To

http://healthylivinghowto.com/

A website that works to provide a "how-to" guide to healthier living.

HealthyChildren.org

http://www.healthychildren.org/english/healthy-living/

An online resource to help provide parents with information on how to ensure that their children are leading a safe and healthy life.

Food Network – Healthy Eating

http://www.foodnetwork.com/healthy-eating/

The food outlet's online resource that provides information on cooking and eating in a healthier manner.

Healthy Food in Health Care

http://www.healthyfoodinhealthcare.org/

A program that provides resources and support to health care facilities.

Food.com

http://healthy.food.com/

A website that provides healthy recipes and tips for home cooking that is nutritional.

Green Smoothie Girl

http://greensmoothiegirl.com/

A website that provides "get healthy" articles and coaching to lead a nutritionally healthier life.

Incredible Smoothies

http://www.incrediblesmoothies.com/green-smoothie-recipes/

A website that provides green smoothie recipes as well as information to improve your overall health.

The Raw Foods Witch

http://rawfoodswitch.com/

A website that offers recipes and commentary to make it easier to lead a raw foods lifestyle.

One Green Planet – "Juicing or Smoothies? Which Are Better?"

http://www.onegreenplanet.org/vegan-health/juicing-or-smoothies-which-are-better/

A website that offers tips to leading a greener lifestyle, through health, food, and even other lifestyle activities like conservation.

Healthy Eating Starts Here

http://www.healthyeatingstartshere.com/nutrition/green-smoothie-benefits

A website that provides recipes and other resources to help get users started on leading a healthy lifestyle and eating foods that are healthy.

WebMD: Living Healthy

http://www.webmd.com/living-healthy

The popular online "doctor" site's guide to leading a healthier life through diet and exercise.

Everyday Health

http://www.everydayhealth.com/

A website that provides information on ensuring that your body is healthy; offers tips on how to better your health.

Today's Dietician

http://www.todaysdietandnutrition.com/

A website that provides recipes, nutrition, and diet information through their health and wellness center.

Total Raw Food

http://www.totalrawfood.com/

A website that offers everything raw food: articles, recipes, events, and products.

RECIPE INDEX

Adrenal Support Smoothie, 154

Apple & Carrot Green Smoothie, 110

Apple & Cucumber Detox Green Smoothie, 75

Apple & Lemon Green Smoothie, 101

Apple & Melon Smoothie, 113

Apple & Pear Power Green Smoothie, 100

Beet It Green Smoothie, 104

Berry & Cabbage Green Smoothie, 69

Berry & Melon Green Smoothie, 46

Berry Basil Green Smoothie, 87

Berry Rocket Green Smoothie, 50

Blackberry & Apple Crunch Green Smoothie, 97

Blackberry & Date Green Smoothie, 66

Blackberry & Seed Green Smoothie, 88

Blackberry Blue Green Smoothie, 84

Blackberry Burst Green Smoothie, 83

Blue Banana Green Smoothie, 43

Blueberry Ice Cream Smoothie, 147

Blueberry Nut Smoothie, 125

Body Boosting Green Smoothie, 108

Breakfast Filler Green Smoothie, 63

Breakfast Treat Green Smoothie, 79

Broccoli Boost Green Smoothie, 98

Brussels Sprout Green Smoothie, 106

Cacao Green Smoothie, 45

Cashew Cream Smoothie, 153

Cherry Berry Smoothie, 119

Cherry Top Green Smoothie, 70

Choccy Ginger Banana Smoothie, 150

Choco Passion Green Smoothie, 57

Choco Peach Green Smoothie, 86

Chocolate Blueberry Green Smoothie, 95

Chocolate Boost Green Smoothie, 131

Cinnamon Apple Smoothie, 149

Cinnamon Treat Green Smoothie, 80

Coco Mango Smoothie, 122

Cocoa Banana Smoothie, 134

Coffee & Almond Breakfast Smoothie, 137

Creamy Peanut Butter Berry Smoothie, 143

Dandelion & Apple Green Smoothie, 82

Detox & Cleansing Smoothie, 155

Fennel Fantastic Green Smoothie, 105

Fruity Power Green Smoothie, 62

Fruity Punch Smoothie, 129

Grapefruit & Pineapple Diet Yogurt Smoothie, 133

Green Snack Smoothie, 65

Heart Health Smoothie, 155

Hot Green Smoothie, 89

Jam Smoothie, 141

Kiwi Paradise Green Smoothie, 102

Lunchtime Booster Green Smoothie, 64

Lunchtime Survival Green Smoothie, 94

Mango Mint Green Smoothie, 71

Melon Berry Yogurt Smoothie, 128

Mint Choc Chip Green Smoothie, 76

Minty Berry Green Smoothie, 72

Mixed Nut & Oat Smoothie, 153

Morning Wake Up Green Smoothie, 93

Muesli Smoothie, 152

Omega 3 Boost Smoothie, 151

Orange & Go Green Smoothie, 55

Orange & Plum Green Smoothie, 68

Papaya Strawberry Smoothie, 116

Parsley & Blueberry Detox Green Smoothie, 77

Passion & Mango Smoothie, 118

Passion Fruit Experience Green Smoothie, 99

Pecan & Macadamia Smoothie, 153

Peach & Almond Smoothie, 124

Pear Delicious Green Smoothie, 51

Pineapple & Nectarine Energy Smoothie, 126

Pineapple Detox Green Smoothie, 47

Pom Berry Smoothie, 121

Pomegranate & Strawberries Smoothie, 145

Pomegranate Green Smoothie, 91

Pumpkin Protein Smoothie, 151

Quick Cold Fix Green Smoothie, 107

Quick Green Smoothie, 53

Quick Orange Breakfast Green Smoothie, 54

Salad Smoothie, 138

Spicy Veg Smoothie, 152

Strawberry & Melon Delight Green Smoothie, 59

Strawberry Cream Green Smoothie, 136

Strawberry Grapefruit Detoxifying Smoothie, 111

Sunflower Satisfying Smoothie, 151

Sweet Green Smoothie, 58

Sweet Pear Smoothie, 115

Sweet Yogurt & Watermelon Smoothie, 144

Thyroid Support Smoothie, 154

Tomato Cream Green Smoothie, 81

Tropical Green Smoothie, 60

Tropical Sweet Green Smoothie, 78

Veggie Virgin Smoothie, 152

Wake Up Green Smoothie, 61

Watermelon Green Smoothie, 73

Wintry Green Smoothie, 132

Zingy Spring Green Smoothie, 48

NOTES